LAST-MINUTE
PATCHWORK + QUILTED GIFTS

LAST-MINUTE

PATCHWORK +
QUILTED GIFTS

JOELLE HOVERSON

PHOTOGRAPHS BY ANNA WILLIAMS

STC CRAFT | A MELANIE FALICK BOOK | NEW YORK

Published in 2007 by Stewart, Tabori & Chang
An imprint of Harry N. Abrams, Inc.

Text copyright © 2007 by Joelle Hoverson
Photographs copyright © 2007 by Anna Williams

Library of Congress Cataloging-in-Publication Data
Hoverson, Joelle. Last-minute patchwork & quilted gifts / By Joelle Hoverson.
p. cm.
Includes index.
ISBN-13: 978-1-58479-634-3
ISBN-10: 1-58479-634-0
1. Patchwork. 2. Quilting. 3. Gifts. I. Title.
TT835.H68 2007
746.46′041—dc22
2006101857

Editor: Melanie Falick
Designer: Brooke Hellewell Reynolds
Production Manager: Jacqueline Poirier

The text of this book was composed in Avenir

Printed and bound in China

10 9 8 7 6 5 4 3

harry n. abrams, inc.
a subsidiary of La Martinière Groupe
115 West 18th Street
New York, NY 10011
www.hnabooks.com

To Anna, Brooke, and Kelly.
Without your friendship and generosity,
this book would not exist.

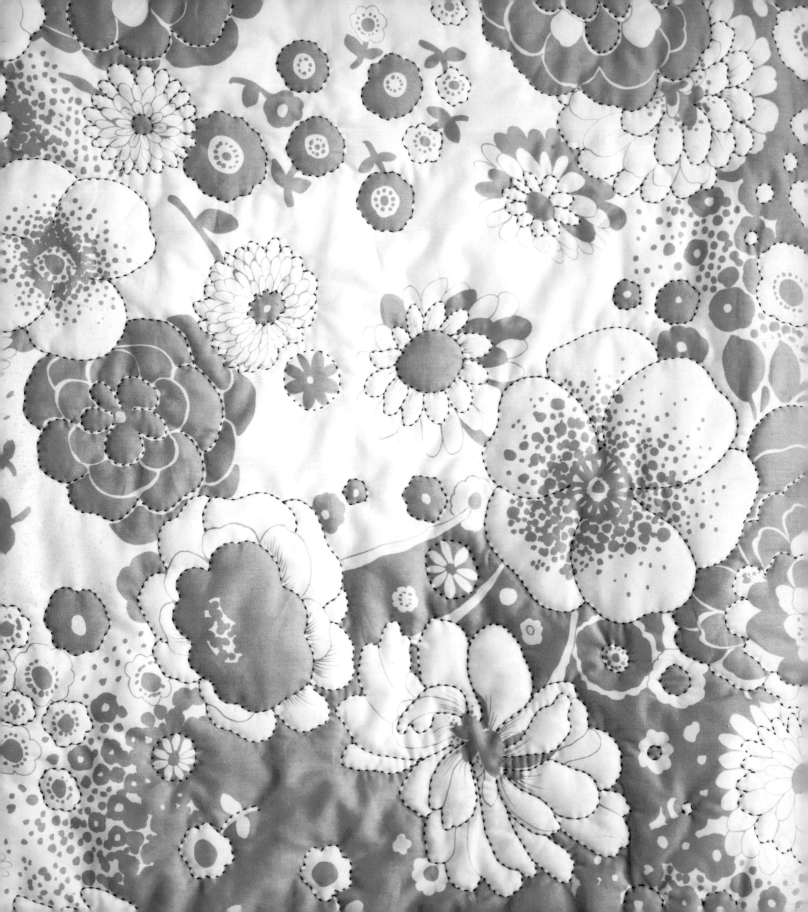

contents

introduction

A few years ago I wrote a book called *Last-Minute Knitted Gifts*. When an editor from Stewart, Tabori & Chang contacted me about writing it, I was surprised and delighted—and a bit intimidated! When that same editor offered me the opportunity to write this book, I was again delighted (and a little less intimidated) because I love creating and giving patchwork and quilted gifts as much as I love knitting gifts for the special people in my life.

The tradition of giving quilts dates back to the early days of our foremothers, when communities came together to create elaborate quilts for weddings, births, and other commemorative events. These days few of us have enough time to create such elaborate gifts; yet our wish to express ourselves through this type of stitchery remains the same. For that reason, I am happy to present this collection of patchwork and quilted projects that draw upon that same spirit of creativity and generosity but fit the time constraints of our modern lifestyles, projects that we can get to and even finish on time.

As I worked on this book, I made many discoveries about who I am as a quilter. I like to have a clear idea of my project before I start; however, it often changes as I go along. My ideas are enriched when I pay attention to how the fabrics are (or aren't) working together and then adapt them accordingly. And I always feel excited when I can figure out a shortcut that doesn't sacrifice the quality of the finished piece. The projects in this book reflect my love of color, pattern, and textiles, and are organized according to how long they take to make. If you are new to patchwork and quilting, I recommend that you give

yourself as much time as possible to finish each project so that you can enjoy the process, but be assured that the projects in the first chapter can be finished very quickly even if you are a beginner. I've tried to be accurate about the time it takes to make each project in the other four chapters as well.

I own two shops in New York City – Purl, a yarn shop, and Purl Patchwork, a fabric shop. At Purl Patchwork, customers often ask me to explain the difference between patchwork and quilting. Patchwork refers to an item made of two or more fabrics that are sewn together to create a visual pattern on the surface. Quilting refers to the stitching that holds three layers of fabric together (the top piece is often patchwork, the middle is usually cotton batting, and the bottom piece is usually a plain piece of fabric). Patchwork can be an element of a quilt (or another object), and a quilt does not always involve patchwork if it is made of a whole cloth (see Follow-the-

Lines Baby Quilt on page 104). Because quilting can be time-consuming, you will notice that projects at the front of the book are almost exclusively patchwork whereas projects toward the end involve both patchwork and quilting. To use this book, either pick out your favorite projects and make the time to work on them, or consider how much time you have available, then look through the projects in the appropriate chapters. If you find you can't finish a more elaborate project in time for a special occasion, consider taking scraps from it and sewing them into something small, like the journal covers on page 30, to give your recipient a taste of what is to come.

I trained as a painter, and one of my great passions in life is color. For me, making a quilt or patchwork project is almost always an exploration of color. Exploring Color, which begins on page 11, is my way of inviting you into this process and, hopefully, inspiring you to embark on your own color journey. In the Patchwork + Quilting Basics section starting on page 127, I explain quilting terminology and techniques as well as materials and tools. I've tried to lay out clear definitions of common terms and directions for following the rules that seem essential, and I've thrown in a few of my favorite shortcuts, too. Nonetheless, this chapter is by no means all-inclusive, so I recommend that you explore some of the wonderful how-to books that have been published (see a list of my favorites on page 154). There are infinite ways to approach patchwork and quilting. In each pattern I've specified the techniques I used, but don't feel that my way is the only way. Pick and choose the methods that suit your style.

Part of the pleasure of patchwork and quilting is exploring its deep roots within so many different cultures. I always find inspiration in the work of quiltmakers who clearly understand the rules and conventions of traditional quilt-ing but who use those conventions as a leaping-off point to discover their own quilting "voices." I am particularly inspired by the quilts of Gee's Bend, Japanese quilts, Hawaiian quilts, and Amish crib quilts. Gee's Bend is a small Alabama community geographically isolated by a winding river and populated by the descendants of for-mer slaves. The quilts of Gee's Bend share an underlying language with traditional patchwork quilts; but, as a result of their geographic and economic isolation, the work of these quiltmakers evolved into a vernacular style that is both unique and inspiring. These quilts are characterized by informal piecing techniques, are almost exclusively made with remnants and hand-me-down fabrics, and are typically quilted with large, uneven stitching; and yet they are nothing less than astonishing in their beauty and spirit. Japanese quilts, if it were actually possible to view them as one uniform idea, can most simply be understood as the opposite aesthetic of the Gee's Bend quilts. They are often exquisitely formal, with subtle color and precise, tiny quilting. Hawaiian quilts are a world unto themselves. Quilting came to Hawaii in the mid-1800s, and the indigenous people of Hawaii soon transformed quilting techniques adopted from the colonists into a unique tradition of their own. In Hawaii, quilters make incredibly complex and large appliqué designs based on the forms of nature, usually from only one piece of cloth cut similarly to paper snowflakes. In the Hawaiian tradition, the design of each quilt is unique and imbued with spiritual meaning. The small scale of the Amish crib quilts seems to have inspired their makers to be more playful and loose with their color combinations and quilting patterns than in their more typically plain-spoken large quilts. And yet these quilts retain the incredible presence of their full-sized counterparts.

Like painting and knitting, making patchwork and quilted projects constantly engages my imagination. I love piecing fabric together to create something special, whether I am creating a small toy, bag, blanket, or wall hanging. Choosing fabrics, pondering prints, and seeing how the colors interact when I sew the pieces together challenges my sense of color and delights my eyes. It's amazing to think about all of the stitchers all over the world, past and present, who have engaged in this same process. The roots of quilting are deep. And it's wonderful to know that what we make—whether it takes just a few hours or much longer—can be lived with, used, and treasured for years to come by the people who are special to us.

exploring color

For me, making patchwork and quilted projects is a wonderful way to play with the elements of color and print, and putting the two together is an exciting adventure. Customers are drawn to the colorful collection of fabrics lining the shelves at Purl Patchwork, but are sometimes uncertain about making color choices. I try to offer them gentle guidance so they can learn to enjoy the process as much as I do. And now I offer the same tools for navigation to you right here.

The Color Wheel

The concept of the color wheel is a useful tool in shaping our understanding of how colors relate to each other, and it can help to guide our color ideas, decisions, and inspirations. On a very basic color wheel, the three primary colors—red, yellow, and blue—are equidistant from each other. Between the primary colors lie the secondary colors: Between red and yellow is orange; between yellow and blue is green; between blue and red is violet. On a more elaborate color wheel (see right), you see shades of each primary and secondary color between these colors: Between red and orange you find orangish-red and then reddish-orange; between orange and yellow, you find yellowish-orange and then orangish-yellow, and so forth. Colors next to one another on the color wheel are "related" colors, and the relationship between them is very harmonious and rich, whereas colors directly across from one another are "complementary" colors, and the relationship between them is very active and dynamic.

Working with Prints and Colors

When you're working with printed fabrics, the simple relationships between related colors and complementary colors become much more complex. Prints can make color relationships more vital. Rather than getting caught up in the theme of prints (such as putting flowers with other flowers, dots with stripes, and so forth), I encourage you to look at prints first and foremost as adding dimension and depth to color. Usually, a printed fabric will have a dominant color, a dull or bright feeling, and a busy or subtle print. Depending on what you are looking for in your project, you can play with all of these aspects. Large-scale prints lend movement and openness, fine prints create a more subtle feeling of depth, and completely solid fabrics give your eye a place to rest.

I made the Color-Wheel Quilt at left as a playful illustration of a color wheel. It is composed of printed fabrics in shades of primary and secondary colors with a solid

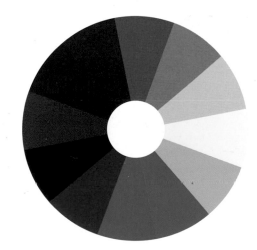

Left: Color-Wheel Quilt, page 107
Right: A "true" color wheel

white background. The difference between a "true" color wheel and my quilt is both important and instructive. A true color wheel begins with "true" primary colors, and the secondary colors are literally the steps between them. On my quilt, the colors don't flow perfectly from one shade to the next; some seem bright, some more dull. For this quilt, I wanted a lot of movement in the color-wheel part of the quilt, so I used both large- and small-scale prints for the colors. The solid white background is spacious and calm, setting off the cheerful business of the colors.

When you're working with predyed and printed fabrics, there is no saying what is a "true" color, and, in fact, a true color should be considered nothing more than a concept. This might seem picky or academic, but it is also precisely where the fun comes in! Colors that fall exactly into order can be very predictable and even boring. When I selected each of the fifty-two fabrics for this quilt, I really enjoyed finding relationships between each color and print that seemed compelling and animated. I didn't fret over finding the literal next step between the colors and prints, and the result is this joyful celebration of color.

Finding the Color Behind the Color
No exploration of color would be complete without some discussion of tertiary colors, which include brown and gray, two wonderfully rich and complex colors. The best way to understand tertiary colors is to get some paints and start mixing them together. Grays are made by mixing together complementary colors—the opposites on the color wheel. There is red-green gray, yellow-violet

gray, and blue-orange gray. Depending on how much of each complement you mix together, you can create a very wide range of grays. Brown is a close cousin of gray. To make brown with your box of paints, you would begin by mixing together equal amounts of the primary colors: red, yellow, and blue. Once you start playing with the proportions of the three primaries, you will begin to find a very large spectrum of browns as well.

Because their qualities can seem more mysterious than the primary and secondary colors, the tertiary colors are a great place to begin to learn about what I like to call "finding the color behind the color." This process of looking deeply helps you to discover what a color is made of. Knowing what colors are made of gives you the ability to create sensitive relationships between them.

Let's take brown, as an example. Pick a range of browns and place them next to one another. If you look carefully, you will begin to see that each brown reveals an underlying color in relation to the others. Some will look more red, some more orange, some more yellow, some green, some blue, and some violet. The underlying color is the color behind the color. When you place the browns together, your eye and brain naturally try to distinguish between them, and their differences become illuminated.

Pieced Pillows, page 37

Left: Little Bits, page 90
Below: Six of One, a Half-Dozen
of the Other, page 80

Finding the color behind the color can help you work with primary and secondary colors, too, even those with very bold prints. When I found the red peony fabric for the Six-of-One, a Half-Dozen of the Other quilt below, I knew I had to find another red fabric to put with it that had a similar underlying orangish-red color, or else the project would be too overwhelming. I looked at the peony fabric with a wide range of other reds until I found just the right one. Because the two reds have the same underlying color, the hot pink, blue, and yellow peonies stand out and sparkle. A very different example of this technique is the Simple Bag on page 14. This project involves two very bold prints in complementary colors. I started by selecting the orange-on-orange pod fabric. When I placed this fabric with lots of other orange fabrics, I could see that it was very earthy, with its underlying color a greenish brown. So I paired it with a fabric with a lot of green in it, which also happened to have a golden brown background that felt related to the color behind the color of the orange pod fabric. The result is a color relationship that, to my eye, glows and harmonizes.

It's like wearing eyeglasses with colored lenses. If you put on your favorite pair of rose-colored glasses, everything you look at will be tinted by the rose lenses, but you will still be able to distinguish between colors. This happens because, after a moment, your brain edits out the rosiness—even if the lenses are quite dark. The more you experiment with this process, the more you'll see.

I put this technique into action when I put the colors together for both the Pieced Pillows at left and the Little Bits quilt above, but with two very different results. When I looked at the dark brown fabric I selected for the pillows with a range of other browns, it revealed itself to be very green. Because green's complement is red, I paired this brown with some very vivid fabrics in the red family. The intense color of the reds and the green undertones of the brown together create a stunning visual relationship that seems almost electric. The dark brown I selected for the Little Bits quilt revealed itself to have blue as its most dominant underlying color. For this project, I wanted to create something very calm, so I paired my brown with prints in a range of blues. While the blues still shine out of the brown background of the quilt, they also relate to it in a way that is both peaceful and serene.

Your Turn

You can take your inspiration from many sources, perhaps a vintage quilt, a beautiful leaf, a painting, or a favorite fabric. Whatever it is, focusing your inspiration before you start can yield a more coherent and exciting project, one that will be admired and appreciated by anyone who receives it. If you know something about the recipient, you can also begin there. Does the recipient have a favorite color, a modern sensibility, or a classic home? Is he or she passionate about gardening, wildlife, or hiking through rain forests? Considering details like these can personalize your quilted gift in subtle, beautiful ways.

Perhaps you want to make a quilt for your sister, who lives in a home that is entirely modern and monochromatic but who is also drawn to bright, delicious colors. You could pick out several fabrics in a range of creams, tans, taupes, and beiges, but finish the back of the quilt in a wild and vibrant violet. On the other hand, if you're making a toy for a newborn whose parents love to travel, you could stitch this child an elephant with a collection of spicy-colored prints that may remind them of a recent trip to India. Your color choices can also let you make your own mark on someone else's gift. Let's say you're making a bag for a friend who only wears black—but you love working with color. You can make the outside and straps of the bag coordinate with her wardrobe, and line the inside with several shades of luscious, velvety red. Whatever the case, the more you try to create a combination of colors and prints that relate to the passions of your recipient and your relationship to him or her, the more special and treasured the gift will be.

Having some knowledge about color and print will help your projects sing and sparkle; but, above all, to successfully combine these elements, the most fundamental step you can take is also the most basic: Look carefully at your project as you make it. When pulling together fabrics, look at everything that interests you as a whole and then decide whether to edit your selection, move things around, or add another choice. Look carefully at what pleases you in order to discover your personal voice. Be assured that, whether your interest is in playing with related or complementary colors, creating movement or stillness, achieving dissonance or harmony, there is no right or wrong answer. All that matters is that it works for you and will be meaningful to the recipient of your gift.

Simple Bag, page 40

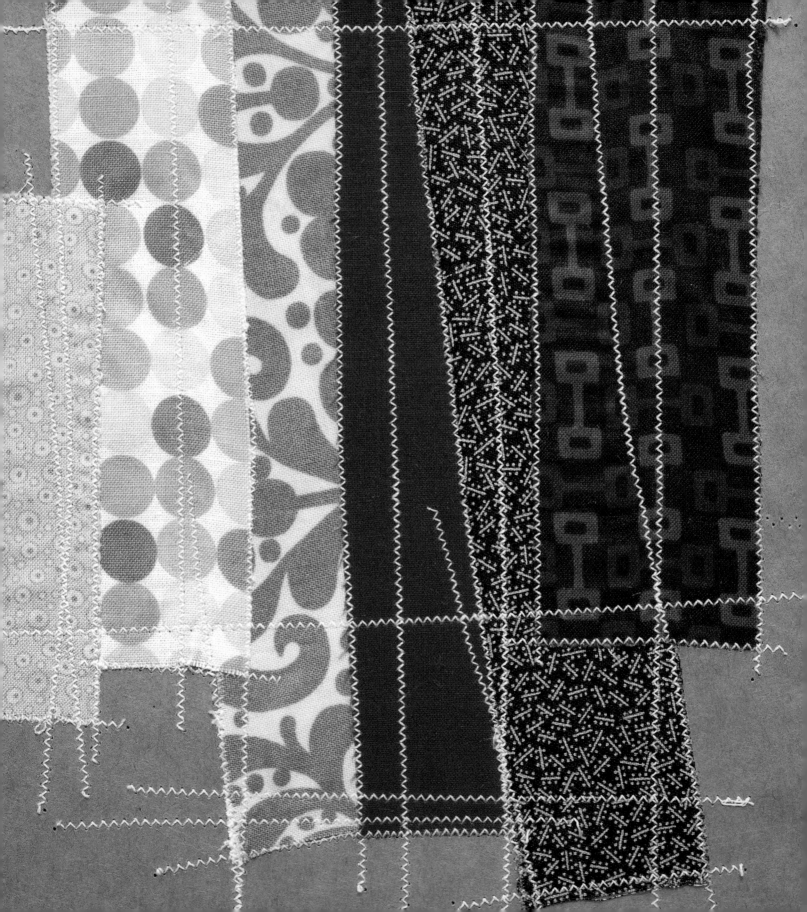

less-than-2-hour gifts

To Molly
Love, Phyllis

on pins
and
needles

on pins + needles

These little needle books take almost no time to make and are very useful for anyone who sews. If you have a group of friends who like to get together for quilting or sewing, you can make one for each person. To wrap as shown in the photo, place the book between two pieces of brightly colored tissue paper and machine-sew around the edges using brightly colored thread. (Be careful not to sew through the project, of course!) Then trim the ends of the tissue paper with pinking shears. This wrapping technique can be used for any small project.

FINISHED MEASUREMENTS
Approximately 4 inches x 3¼ inches (closed)

MATERIALS
(FOR ONE BOOK)
8½-inch x 11-inch piece of printable cotton fabric, for label (see Sources for Supplies, page 156)

Plant-dyed wool felt, at least 4 inches x 6½ inches, for cover (see Sources for Supplies, page 156)

Off-white cotton flannel for pages, three pieces at least 3½ inches x 6 inches each (*Note: ¼ yard of flannel will make enough pages for three books.*)

Cotton thread in a bright, contrasting color

One or more heavy-duty denim sewing-machine needles (*Note: Wool felt dulls the needle very quickly, so keep extra needles on hand if you're making more than one book.*)

Walking foot for sewing machine

1. Make Label for Cover
Following the manufacturer's directions, print a label for your book on one sheet of printable-cotton fabric. (Even if you're only making one book, you may want to print a whole page of labels in bright colors for later use). After printing, remove the fabric's backing, and wash it in soapy water. You can wash the fabric by hand and let it air-dry, or you can machine-wash and tumble it dry. (*Note: If you don't wash the fabric, it will scorch when ironed.*) Cut the label(s) to your desired size and set them aside.

2. Cut Felt
Cut felt into 4-inch x 6½-inch rectangles, one for each book.

3. Make Pages
Cut the flannel into three 3½-inch x 6-inch pieces. (If you're cutting fabric for a few books from a ¼ yard of fabric, cut a 6-inch-deep strip from selvage to selvage, trim off the selvage edges, and then cut the strip into nine 3½-inch x 6-inch pieces. These will be enough for three books.) Align and layer three pieces of flannel on top of one another, and set the unit aside.

4. Assemble Book
Position the label on the felt front cover, and machine-sew it into place with a small zigzag stitch. Stitch around the label twice to ensure that all its edges are secure and to make the thread color more visible.

Turn the felt cover face down, and center the flannel pages over it, leaving approximately ¼ inch of felt showing all around the flannel.

Using the walking foot on your machine and a straight stitch, sew down the middle of all four layers of fabric to create a "spine," backstitching (see page 142) at the beginning and end of your stitching to secure your seam.

quilted coasters

These coasters make a great housewarming gift. Each one takes about 15 minutes to complete, so it's easy to plan on making a set of four or six for a generous gift. I chose some 19th-century reproduction fabrics for this project. I like the way the small scale of the prints complements the small size of the coasters and the fine sewn lines of the concentric rectangles of quilting.

FINISHED MEASUREMENTS
Approximately 4 inches square

MATERIALS
4½-inch x 10-inch piece fabric for each coaster (*Note: ¼ yard of 44-inch-wide fabric will yield eight coasters if cut precisely.*)

Fabric scissors

High-loft, natural cotton batting, 46 inches x 36 inches

Cotton thread in color to blend with most of your fabrics (I used mustard yellow)

Walking foot for sewing machine

CONSTRUCTION NOTES
Use ¼-inch seam allowance throughout, unless otherwise noted.

1. Prepare Fabric
Wash, dry, and press the fabric.

2. Cut Fabric
Cut one 4½-inch x 10-inch piece of fabric for each coaster. (If you're making coasters from ¼ yard of fabric, cut two 4½-inch-deep strips from selvage to selvage, trim the selvages, and then cut each strip into four 10-inch lengths.)

3. Cut Batting
Cut one 4-inch square of batting for each coaster.

4. Assemble Coaster
Fold the fabric in half, right sides together, to form a 4½-inch x 5-inch rectangle. Sew the two 5-inch sides closed, so that only one side of the rectangle remains open. You don't need to backstitch these seams because you'll be sewing over them when you quilt your coaster. (*Note: If you're making more than one coaster, you can chain-piece [see page 143] these side seams to save time.*) Trim the corners, and turn the fabric right side out.

Tuck the batting smoothly inside the fabric (this can be a bit fussy at first, but it gets easier with practice). Fold the coaster's open edges to the inside, covering the batting with one fabric edge, and finger-press (see page 144) the folded edges in place. Make the corners as square as possible. Your piece should measure approximately 4 inches square.

5. Quilt Coaster
Attach the walking foot to your sewing machine, and set your machine to the needle-down position in order to cleanly turn each corner as you quilt. (If your machine cannot be set this way, hand-turn your needle into the down position before lifting the presser foot to turn the coaster at the corners.)

Wrap a set of coasters together with a recipe and supplies for iced tea for a special summer house-warming gift.

You'll start quilting at the outside edge and sew in one continuous line to the center. Use the coaster's edge as a guide to make straight seams the first time around, and then continue using the outer seams as your guide as you work your way inward. Begin quilting about ⅛ inch from the edge on a side neighboring the open edge (you'll close the open edge when you quilt along that side). Sew a few stitches, then take a couple backstitches to anchor the quilting. Stitch along the side of the coaster, consistently staying about ⅛ inch from the edge.

At the first corner, stop sewing with your needle in the down position. Lift the presser foot, and rotate the coaster 90 degrees; lower the presser foot, and sew to the next corner. Repeat stitching along each side and turning the corner as instructed until you're on the fourth side, then stop sewing ¼ inch before you reach the last corner. ★ With your needle in the down position, lift the presser foot and rotate the coaster 90 degrees; lower the presser foot, and sew ¼ inch inside the previous stitching line to within ¼ inch of the next corner.

Repeat the process from ★ above to form concentric rectangles of quilting until you reach the center of the piece. Finish the quilting with a few backstitches.

simple pillowcases

Custom-made pillowcases can easily become the centerpiece in a beautifully designed bedroom. These pillowcases are very simple to make. If I'm feeling really generous, I give them with a handmade quilt (see Log Cabin Quilt, page 120), but they also make a great gift on their own.

FINISHED MEASUREMENTS
18½ inches x 30 inches

(Note: The finished dimensions are based on a standard purchased pillowcase. To make a 20-inch x 40-inch king-size pillowcase, use the measurements given in parentheses, if they're different.)

MATERIALS (FOR ONE PILLOWCASE)

FABRIC 1: ¾ yard (1 yard) of 45-inch-wide floral cotton, for main fabric

FABRIC 2: ½ yard of 45-inch-wide solid cotton, for contrasting fabric

Cotton thread to match contrasting fabric

CONSTRUCTION NOTES
Use ⅛-inch seam allowance when top-stitching seams, and ½-inch seam allowances elsewhere.

1. Prepare Fabric
Wash, dry, and press the fabric.

2. Cut Fabric
From Fabric 1, cut a 25-inch-deep x 38-inch-wide (35-inch-deep x 41-inch-wide) rectangle. From Fabric 2, cut a 13-inch-deep x 38-inch-wide (13-inch-deep x 41-inch-wide) rectangle.

3. Make Pillowcase
With right sides together, align and pin the two fabrics together along their 38-inch (41-inch) edge. Then sew the two fabrics together along this pinned edge. Press the seam to the contrasting fabric's side.

With right sides together, fold together the long edges of the newly joined piece to form a 19-inch x 37-inch (20½-inch x 47-inch) rectangle. Align, pin, and sew the 37-inch (47-inch) edges together, backstitching at the beginning and end of the seam. Press the seam open.

Align and pin the edges of Fabric 1's 19-inch (20½-inch) side, and sew this edge, backstitching at the beginning and end of the seam. You don't need to press this seam.

On Fabric 2's 19-inch (20½-inch) side, fold the cut edge ½ inch to the wrong side of the pillowcase, and press the fold.

Fold the outer half of the contrasting fabric to the pillowcase's wrong side, aligning the folded edge with the first seam you sewed so this end of pillowcase consists of a double fold of fabric. Pin the folded edge in place all the way around the seam, and topstitch the folded edge in place ⅛ inch from the fold.

Turn the pillowcase right side out, and press it.

bird ornaments

FINISHED MEASUREMENTS
Approximately 4½ inches from
tip of beak to tail

MATERIALS
Approximately 6-inch-square
piece of patterned fabric,
for main body of bird

Approximately 10-inch x
4-inch piece of coordinating
patterned fabric, for bird's
belly and hanging loop (*Note:
¼ yard of each fabric will yield
a small flock of birds.*)

Cotton thread to match
main body fabric

Natural cotton stuffing

Fabric scissors

½-inch tape maker

Hand-sewing needle

Crochet hook size D or smaller
(or similar blunt tool for turning
bird right side out)

Heavy-duty template plastic,
at least a 6-inch square

Fine-tip permanent marker

Pattern Templates A and B
(from pattern sheet attached
to inside back cover of book)

CONSTRUCTION NOTES
Use ¼-inch seam allowances
throughout.

To lend these birds sweet old-fashioned charm, I made
them using reproductions of 19th-century brown and pink
fabrics. Each bird takes about 45 minutes to make from
start to finish.

1. Prepare Fabric
Wash, dry, and press the fabrics.

2. Make Fabric Loop
Cut one ¾-inch x 10-inch strip from the coordinating fabric and set aside the
leftover fabric for the bird belly (if you're making more than one bird with
¼ yard of fabric, cut a ¾-inch-deep strip from selvage to selvage, which will
make four loops). Use a ½-inch bias tape maker to create a perfectly folded
strip, pressing the fabric immediately as it comes out of the tape maker.

Once you've pressed the fabric strip, fold the two outer edges together and
press the folded strip again to create a ¼-inch-wide folded strip, with the cut
edges hidden inside. Machine-sew the strip closed, stitching as close as possible to the outer edge. Trim the strip to 8 inches, and set it aside.

3. Make Templates
Instead of cutting out TEMPLATES A and B directly from the pattern sheet
page attached to inside back cover of book, trace the pieces onto template
plastic, and cut them out. Then you'll still have all the templates in one place,
should you ever want to use them again.

4. Cut Shapes
Fold the main body fabric in half, right sides together. Place TEMPLATE A
(the bird body) on the fabric, and trace around the template with a pencil;
then pin the two fabric layers together, and cut along the marked lines. Set
the cut pieces aside.

Fold the bird belly fabric in half, with right sides together and its 4-inch edges
aligned. Position the straight edge of TEMPLATE B (the belly) on the fabric's
folded edge, and trace around the template with a pencil. Pin the fabric layers
together, and cut along the marked line; then open up the cut pattern piece.

5. Sew Bird

✱ With the right sides of the fabric together, pin the belly fabric along the bottom edge of one side of the bird body, using lots of pins to ease the curved shapes together; you want the points at the beak and tail of both pieces to meet. Sew along the pinned edge from beak to tail. (There's no need to back-stitch because you'll reinforce the seam when you sew the other side of the body to the belly.) Be sure to keep the curved stitching line smooth as you sew so that your bird will be nice and rounded.

Repeat from ✱ to attach the second half of bird body to the belly, but this time leave a gap about 1½ inches long in the center of the seam for turning the bird right side out and stuffing it. Tip: when you make the 1½-inch open-ing, you don't need to break or cut the thread. Just lift the needle and presser foot, draw out some extra thread from the spool and bobbin, position the fabric 1½ inches down the seamline, lower your presser foot, and resume sewing. You can clip this extra thread in the opening before you turn your bird right side out. Be careful not to sew over the opposite side of the bird on this second seam!

6. Attach Loop

Fold the completed loop in half, stacking the ends on top of each other. With the bird body still turned wrong side out, slide the folded loop into the body where marked on **TEMPLATE A**, letting the loop's stacked ends extend ½ inch beyond the seamline of the body. Pin the stacked ends in place.

To avoid stitching over the loop when you sew the top seam, draw the loop through the opening on the side of the bird's body. Sew together the body's top edge from tip to tail, taking care not to sew over the nice points you made at the ends of the previous seams. Your top seam should just intersect the point where the previous seams meet.

7. Turn Bird Right Side Out

Because the beak and tail both come to sharp points, turning them out is a bit fiddly. Trim the seam allowance at each end to about ⅛ inch, being careful not to cut too close to the stitches (which could make your seams come apart when you stuff the bird). Turn the bird right side out; and, using the blunt end of a small crochet hook or a similar tool, push the beak and tail points out-wards. If you can't get the points pushed all the way out, coax them from the outside with a pin, and then use the end of the crochet hook again from the inside. Repeat the process until you're satisfied with the results.

Without the hanging loops, these ornaments also make nice gifts for children; or, if you're feeling a bit sinister, you can always put a little catnip inside one and give it to your kitty!

8. Stuff Bird

Using small pieces of cotton stuffing and the blunt end of the crochet hook, stuff the beak and tail. Continue stuffing the belly until it looks nice and plump.

9. Hand-Sew Opening

Using a blindstitch (see page 144), carefully hand-sew the opening in the bird body closed. For best results, finger-press the fabric (see page 144) to the inside as you sew to create a clean edge and a ¼-inch seam allowance. Sew just inside the fold for an invisible seam.

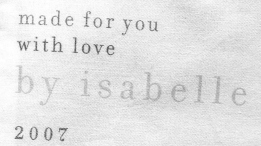

made for you
with love
by isabelle

2007

made-by patch

Quilt historians use many methods for dating and attributing heirloom quilts, but in the end they can only guess unless, of course, the maker stitched her name and the date on the back of her quilt. This patch is a wonderful way to ensure that historians won't be guessing at the origins of your future heirloom! It's also a wonderful final flourish for a special gift.

FINISHED MEASUREMENTS
This patch is about 4 inches square, but you can make yours any size you want.

MATERIALS
8½-inch x 11-inch sheet of printable cotton fabric (see Sources for Supplies on page 156)

Lightweight fusible interfacing for one patch (or as many as you plan to make)

Cotton thread to match quilt back on which you'll sew patch

Small crochet hook or similar blunt tool

Hand-sewing needle

CONSTRUCTION NOTES
Use ¼-inch seam allowances throughout.

1. Make Labels
Following the manufacturer's directions, print one or more labels on one sheet of printable cotton. (Note that, even if you need only one Made-By Patch at a time, you may want to print a whole page of patches—I fit four on a page—for later use.) After printing the fabric, remove its backing, and wash the printed fabric in soapy water. You can wash it in the sink with dish soap and let it air-dry, or you can machine-wash and tumble it dry. (Note that if you don't wash the fabric, it will scorch when ironed.)

2. Make Patch
Press the printed fabric. Cut the patch to your desired size, making sure to include enough room for a ¼-inch seam allowance all around it. Then cut the interfacing to the same size as your patch.

Next, prepare to sew the patch and interfacing together by placing the patch, right side up, and laying the interfacing, fusible side down, on top of the patch. Carefully align the corners of the patch and interfacing, and pin the two in place.

Sew around all four edges, and trim the corners. Then cut an opening in the interfacing wide enough to turn the patch right side out, being sure to cut the opening no closer than 1 inch from the seamline. Turn the patch right side out through this opening. Using a small crochet hook or similar blunt tool, carefully poke out the corners until they are as square as possible.

3. Fuse Patch to Quilt
Position the patch on the back of the quilt, and press it into place (the interfacing will fuse your patch to the back of the quilt). Using a hand-sewing needle, blindstitch (see page 144) the patch to the quilt back by hand. Sew the patch just underneath its folded edge for the most invisible results.

scrapbooks

This is one of my favorite projects. It uses up scraps I can't bear to throw away, allows a certain freedom in color combinations, and is very quick to make. I know a lot of people who don't go anywhere without a notebook, so this project makes both a creative and useful gift. I especially love the utilitarian feel of the Moleskine Cahier notebooks I use. They're easy to sew through, and the brown covers complement most fabrics. I recommend sacrificing at least one journal to the learning process, so you can experiment with thread colors, zigzag-stitch length, and presser-foot pressure without worrying about achieving perfect gift-worthy results.

FINISHED MEASUREMENTS
Varies with the size of your notebook

MATERIALS
Moleskine Cahier Notebook, in any size (see Sources for Supplies, page 156; available in sets of three)

Cotton thread in bright, contrasting color (I used bright yellow)

Various fabric scraps

White glue, such as Elmer's

Hair dryer (optional)

Tip: Once you use a sewing-machine needle on paper, it will be too dull for use on fabric. So if you're planning to make a bunch of these journals, it's worth doing them all at once with the same needle. If you're only making one journal at a time, store the used needle in an envelope marked "For Paper," so you can find and use it again later.

1. Prepare Materials
Set your machine to a small zigzag stitch. Reduce the pressure of the presser foot to keep the fabric from getting bunched up or shifting as you sew.

Assemble your scraps into a pleasing design on the cover of the notebook. To keep the design stable as you're sewing in the next step, I find it helpful to press the assembled fabrics together as a unit with a hot iron before sewing.

2. Anchor Scraps on Notebook Cover
Begin machine-sewing the scraps to the notebook cover with a few long, vertical stitching lines, keeping the fabric as flat as possible as you sew (there's no need to backstitch at the beginning or end of your seams since you'll secure the end of the seam with glue in a moment). Trim the thread tails. Then sew several horizontal lines across the cover, and again trim the thread tails.

3. Sew Edges of Scraps
Once you've stabilized the basic design on the cover, sew along the edge of each fabric scrap to prevent fraying and give your scrapbook a finished look. Trim the thread tails.

Place a small drop of white glue on the inside cover at each end of your stitched lines to secure them. Allow the glue to dry before closing the book! To speed up the process, dry the glue with a hair dryer on a low-heat setting.

2- to 4-hour gifts

flannel baby blanket

This baby blanket is one of the simplest projects in this book. Call me a hopeless romantic, but I think that a hand-finished binding is very special, even though it takes time. I always feel that I'm sealing my gift with love; each stitch is filled with it. The type of binding used here is called a double-fold binding.

FINISHED MEASUREMENTS
Approximately 34 inches x
42 inches

**MATERIALS
(FOR ONE BLANKET)**

1 yard of 45-inch-wide white or off-white cotton flannel (or 1¼ yards of 36-inch-wide flannel)

½ yard of 45-inch-wide printed cotton fabric, for binding

Cotton thread to match flannel

Fabric scissors

Hand-sewing needle

CONSTRUCTION NOTES
Use ¼-inch seam allowances throughout.

1. Prepare Fabric
Wash, dry, and press the fabric.

2. Cut Blanket Fabric
Trim the selvages from the flannel fabric, and square up the sides (see page 139) so that the piece measures about 34 inches x 42 inches. Set it aside.

3. Cut Binding Strips
Fold binding fabric selvage to selvage. Cut five 2¼-inch-deep strips from fold to selvages. Trim the fabric's selvages.

4. Piece and Attach Binding
You'll join the fabric strips to make one long binding strip and then bind the blanket with a double-fold binding, mitering the corners and hand-sewing the folded edge to the blanket's wrong side. You'll find complete directions for piecing the binding strip and making a double-fold binding on page 151.

pieced pillows

FINISHED MEASUREMENTS
Approximately 16 inches square

MATERIALS (FOR FOUR
16-INCH SQUARE PILLOWS)

2¼ yards of 45-inch-wide patterned
cotton fabric, for pillow fronts

¾ yard each of four solid-color,
45-inch-wide cotton accent fabrics,
for strips and pillow backs (I used
two hot pinks and two bright reds)

Four 16-inch-square pillow forms

Cotton thread to match front fabric

Hand-sewing needle

CONSTRUCTION NOTES
Use ¼-inch seam allowances for
piecing pillow front and ½-inch
seam allowances elsewhere.

A NOTE ON PILLOW SIZES
I don't like an overstuffed pillow,
and these directions reflect my
taste. The standard convention is
to use a pillow form 1 inch larger
than the pillowcase. However, these
instructions are written for pillow
forms 1 inch smaller than their
cases, and that is how the pillows
shown in the photograph were
made. Of course, you can modify
the instructions to create whatever
effect you like.

I wanted to make some throw pillows with a modern feel, so I created this design with a graphic sensibility. I love the combination of a dark brown background fabric with vivid pink accent strips, but you can use any combination of colors you like.

1. Prepare Fabric
Wash, dry, and press the fabric.

2. Cut Fabric
From the front fabric, cut four 19-inch squares (the squares will be 3 inches larger than the pillow forms). Set the squares aside.

* Fold one accent fabric in half from selvage to selvage. Trim the selvages, and cut the fabric at the fold to create two 20-inch-wide pieces. Cut one piece down to a 19-inch square, and set it aside. Cut ten ¾-inch strips from the other 20-inch-wide piece. Repeat the process from * for the remaining accent fabrics. You'll then have more than enough strips to play around with for all four pillows.

3. Lay Out Pillow Front
Lay the front fabric right side up, and position several accent strips, right side up, in a pleasing arrangement on top of the fabric. I purposely arranged mine askew to give my pillows a whimsical look. (If you plan to use both vertical and horizontal accent strips, as I did in two of my pillows, first create the vertical strips, working through Step 5, and then repeat Steps 3-5 to add the horizontal strips). Note that you'll be trimming the main fabric down before sewing the pillow front to the back, so don't place any strips closer than 3 inches from the edge of the front fabric.

4. Cut Pillow Front Pieces
To cut the front fabric into the pieces your design requires, begin with the accent strip nearest the front's left side (the strips should still be positioned on the front fabric as you arranged them in Step 3). Place the ruler's edge along one side of the strip (it doesn't matter which side; you'll be making one cut in the main fabric for each accent strip you plan to insert). Using a rotary cutter and the ruler's edge as your guide, cut the main fabric in a straight line from

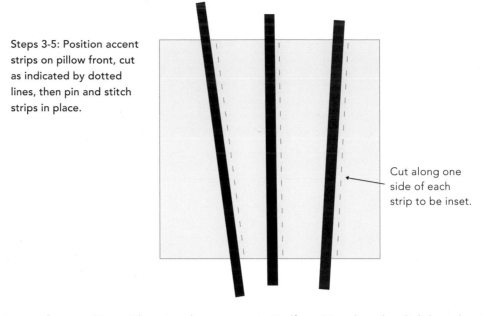

Steps 3-5: Position accent strips on pillow front, cut as indicated by dotted lines, then pin and stitch strips in place.

Cut along one side of each strip to be inset.

top to bottom. (To avoid cutting the accent strip itself, position the ruler slightly to the side of the strip.) Continue cutting the main fabric into pieces, working from left to right across the pillow front and cutting once for every strip arranged over it.

5. Piece Pillow Front

Align and pin both edges of the accent strips to the front-fabric pieces they abut, with right sides together, and sew all the pieces along the pinned edges, (see the diagram above). Press all the seams to the side of the darker fabric. (*Note: If you plan to chain-piece [see page 143] your strips because you're making more than one pillow at a time or you simply want to save a bit of time, it's a good idea to mark the numerical order of the front-fabric pieces to keep them in order when you're sewing and ensure that your final piece is the correct shape.*)

6. Cut Down Pillow Front and Back

Choose one of the accent fabrics for the pillow back. Cut down the pillow front and back to 18-inch squares (each piece will be 2 inches larger than the pillow form's dimensions).

7. Sew Pillow

Align and pin together the pillow's front and back, right sides together. Sew around three sides of the square, beginning and ending with a few backstitches. Trim the corners and turn the pillow right side out. Fold the pillow's open ends ½ inch to the wrong side, and press them in place.

8. Stuff Pillow

Stuff the pillow case with the pillow form. Using a blindstitch (see page 144), carefully hand-sew the remaining opening closed, stitching just inside the fold for the most invisible results.

simple bag

I came up with this bag design to highlight the beauty of the large-scale, modern prints in designer Amy Butler's Forest Collection, a heavyweight, cotton home-decor fabric. I love how the colors in the collection "sing" when they're placed side by side.

FINISHED MEASUREMENTS
Approximately 12 inches x
15 inches

MATERIALS
½ yard printed heavyweight
cotton, for exterior base

½ yard contrasting, printed
heavyweight cotton, for exterior top

½ yard coordinating, printed
heavyweight cotton, for lining

Cotton thread to match
exterior-top fabric

Denim sewing-machine needle

Hand-sewing needle

Heavy-duty straight pins

1-inch tape maker

CONSTRUCTION NOTES
Use ½-inch seam allowances
throughout, except for topstitching.

1. Prepare Fabric
Wash, dry, and press the fabric.

2. Cut Fabric
From the exterior-base fabric, cut one piece measuring 15 inches x 13 inches.

From the exterior-top fabric, cut one 1¾-inch-deep strip from selvage to selvage, and carefully trim away the selvages. Cut one 9-inch-deep strip from selvage to selvage; then cut it into two 9-inch x 13-inch pieces.

From the lining fabric, cut one 13-inch-deep strip from selvage to selvage, then cut it down to one 13-inch x 31-inch piece. Cut one 1¾-inch-deep strip from selvage to selvage, and trim away the selvages.

3. Make Straps
Using the 1-inch tape maker, make a 1-inch strip from each of the 1¾-inch-deep strips you cut from the exterior-top fabric and the lining fabric.

Press and align the strips, wrong sides together, and pin them in place. Topstitch the two strips together with a ⅛-inch seam allowance along both long edges. Cut the stitched strip into two 21-inch-long straps, and set them aside.

4. Sew Exterior
With right sides together, align, pin, and sew one 13-inch edge of the exterior-base fabric to one 13-inch edge of one of the cut pieces of exterior-top fabric. Then, again with right sides together, align, pin, and sew the second 13-inch edge of the exterior-base fabric to one 13-inch edge of the second piece of exterior-top fabric.

Fold the sewn piece in half, with right sides together, across the center of the base fabric, parallel to the seams, to create a 13-inch x 16-inch rectangle. Align the seams and edges, and pin the edges in place. Sew along both 16-inch sides. Press the seams open.

Fold the top open edge of the bag ½ inch to the wrong side, and press. Trim the bottom corners, turn the piece right side out, and set it aside.

5. Sew Lining
Fold the lining fabric in half, right sides together, to form a 13-inch x 16-inch rectangle. Align, pin, and sew both 16-inch sides closed. Press the seams open. Fold the open top edge of the lining ½ inch to the wrong side and press. Trim the corners.

6. Finish Bag
Place the lining inside the bag exterior (with the wrong sides of the lining and bag exterior facing one another), and align and pin the side seams. Pin the straps in place, positioning each one 2½ inches from one of the bag's side seams and with ½ inch of the strap's cut end placed inside the bag between the exterior and lining fabrics. Make sure the straps aren't twisted and that the fabric you want to show is facing out.

Pin the rest of the lining fabric's top edge to the top edge of the bag's exterior. Topstitch around the top edge ¼ inch from the edge. Tack the lining in the bottom corners of the bag by hand to anchor it in place, taking a couple of small stitches that won't show on the bag's exterior.

super quick + easy baby quilt

I always have the best of intentions—as soon as I hear that a friend is pregnant or adopting, I start thinking about what I'll make for the child. But very often, time gets away from me, and I need to create something special in a hurry. This quilt is just right for this situation since it's simple, fun, and fast to make. I wanted the look of a traditional tied quilt but without ties since they wouldn't be safe for a baby. To create this effect, I secured the layers of the quilt with one of the embroidery stitches on my sewing machine. If your machine can't do embroidery, you can substitute a zigzag stitch (I've provided instructions for both options). I chose washable wool batting to make the quilt light, lofty, and easy to launder.

FINISHED MEASUREMENTS
Approximately 34 inches x 41 inches

MATERIALS
1 yard each of two cotton fabrics that look nice together (my front is striped cotton and the back is an alphabet print)

Small spool of thread to blend with both fabrics, for seams

Small spool of contrasting thread, for "ties" (I used medium yellow)

Washable wool batting, 46 inches by 36 inches

CONSTRUCTION NOTES
Use ½-inch seam allowances for quilt assembly; use a machine satin-stitch oval for "ties" (see directions on page 44 for zigzag-stitch alternative if your machine doesn't satin-stitch).

1. Prepare Fabric
Wash, dry, and press the fabric.

2. Cut Fabric
Square up the fabrics (see page 139), trimming off the barest minimum from the sides and selvage edges. Both fabrics should be the same size and no bigger than 46 inches x 36 inches, which is the size of the batting (my fabrics were 42 inches x 35 inches).

3. Cut Batting
Cut one piece of batting to the exact size of your fabric rectangles.

4. Assemble Quilt
Layer the fabrics and batting in this order, from top to bottom: front fabric, right side up; back fabric, wrong side up; batting. Carefully align and pin the edges of all three layers to stabilize them.

Sew all the way around the edges, leaving a 6-inch opening on one of the short sides for turning the quilt right side out. Trim the corners, and turn the piece right side out. Fold the edges on the opening to the inside, with the back fabric folded around the batting. Finger-press (see page 144) the folded edges, and blindstitch (see page 144) the opening by hand.

5. Mark Position of "Ties"

Lightly pencil-mark where you want your satin-stitch ovals to be. I made mine at about 4-inch intervals, starting my rows of ties about 2½ inches in vertically and horizontally from the quilt's edges. (*Note: Check your batting packaging to determine how far apart to position the satin-stitch ovals to ensure that the batting will not shift over time; usually the maximum interval between such stitches is 8 inches.*)

6. Satin-Stitch Ovals

Set your machine for a satin-stitch oval, and thread it with the contrasting thread. It's worth doing a few practice ovals on a fabric scrap before starting on the actual quilt to get a feel for how the stitch works and will look.

Satin-stitch over each pencil mark. You don't have to cut the thread between ovals; just pull some extra thread from the spool and bobbin when you finish an oval, and move on to the next mark. Then trim the threads all at once when you've finished sewing.

ZIGZAG OPTION

If your machine can't do embroidery stitches, try this: Set your machine to a zigzag stitch, at its largest possible width and smallest length. Sew over the pencil mark for about ½ inch, backstitch for the same distance, and then move on to the next mark. Practice on a fabric scrap first to get a feel for this zigzag tie. You don't have to cut the thread between each tie; just pull some extra thread from the spool and bobbin after finishing a zigzag tie, and move on to the next mark. Then trim the threads all at once after you've finished sewing.

kelly's pincushions

My dear friend Kelly McKaig created this pincushion pattern, and I just love the way it looks as well as the way it's put together. Kelly made the original cushion from a vintage eight-pointed star quilt scrap that she found at an antiques mall. She sewed the points together, filled it with sawdust, and a pincushion was born. Kelly always makes the most adorable small projects, and her attention to detail is amazing.

FINISHED MEASUREMENTS
Approximately 4 inches wide x 1½ inches high

MATERIALS
Scraps from 8 different cotton prints, each measuring at least 2½ inches x 5½ inches

Cotton thread that blends with most of fabrics

Fabric scissors

Embroidery thread to complement all fabrics

Embroidery or sashiko needle

Natural cotton stuffing

Template plastic, at least a 6-inch by 3-inch piece

Template C (from pattern sheet page attached to inside back cover of book)

CONSTRUCTION NOTES
Use ¼-inch seam allowances throughout.

1. Prepare Fabric
Wash, dry, and press the fabric.

2. Make Template
Make TEMPLATE C from pattern sheet page attached to inside back cover of book: Instead of cutting the template directly from the page, trace and cut it out of template plastic. Then you'll still have all the templates in one place, should you ever want to use them again.

3. Cut Fabric Shapes

Fold one fabric scrap in half along its width, right sides together. Lay the marked edge of the template along the fabric's folded edge, and trace around the template with the pencil. Cut the fabric on the drawn line, and open up the shape. Repeat this process with the remaining fabric scraps.

4. Chain-Piece Pairs

Pin the cut pieces into pairs, right sides together, carefully aligning the points and edges. Chain-piece (see page 143) the pairs, sewing past the points at each end. You don't need to backstitch because you'll reinforce these seams when sewing the pairs together. Be sure to make smooth curves as you sew, so that your pincushion will be evenly rounded.

After chain-piecing, carefully cut the threads between the pieces to separate them. Press the seams to the side of the darker fabric.

5. Make Half-Spheres
Pair the pieces once more, aligning their cut edges with right sides together, and sew them together to create two half-sphere shapes with four pieces each. Press the seams to the side of the darker fabric.

6. Complete Sphere
Turn one half-sphere right side out, and tuck it inside the other half-sphere, with right sides together. Align the points and edges, and pin the two pieces together. You'll want to begin and end your seam to leave the ½-inch opening indicated on the template for turning the cushion right side out. Sew along the pinned edge, taking care not to sew over the nice points you made at the ends when stitching the previous seams. Your top seam should just intersect the point where the previous seams meet.

7. Stuff and Close Pincushion
Turn the piece right side out through the opening, and stuff it firmly, making a flattish ball. Fold and finger-press (see page 144) the edges of the opening ¼ inch to the inside to create a clean edge. Using a blindstitch (see page 144), carefully hand-sew the opening closed, stitching just inside the fold for an invisible seam.

8. Finish Pincushion
Thread the embroidery or sashiko needle with a 30-inch piece of embroidery thread. Make a quilter's knot (see page 149) at the thread's end. Insert the needle at the base of the cushion, near the intersection of the bottom points, and draw it out at the base intersection, popping the knot to the inside of the cushion (see page 150).

Wrap the thread around the outside of the cushion along one of the seams, insert needle through the intersecting seams at the top of the cushion and out through the bottom. Pull the thread snug, and catch the needle in the wrapped thread at the base of the cushion before wrapping it around the outside of the cushion again, following a different seam on the first half of the cushion. Repeat the wrapping process until you've wrapped the four seams on the first half of the cushion, pulling the thread snugly through the cushion each time. Knot the thread close to the cushion, pulling the needle through and out of the cushion, and popping the knot to the inside of the cushion. Trim the thread tail closely, so it slips inside the cushion. Repeat the above process for the remaining four seams on the other half of the cushion.

Follow Steps 1-5 to make two half-spheres. Turn one half-sphere right side out, as explained in Step 6, and tuck it inside the other, carefully aligning points and edges. Then follow Steps 7 and 8 for finishing.

colored pencil roll

Approximately 9 inches x 24 inches

MATERIALS
24 different cotton prints in a color spectrum that complements your colored pencils (you can use scraps measuring at least 1⅝ inches x 11 inches), for pieced interior

½ yard heavyweight home-decor fabric (I used yarn-dyed cotton from Japan; linen fabric will also work), for exterior and pocket

¼ yard quilter's muslin, for pocket lining

½ yard white or off-white flannel, for batting

1 yard linen twill tape or other ribbon, for ties

Cotton thread to match exterior fabric

Hera marker

Walking foot for sewing machine

CONSTRUCTION NOTES
Use ¼-inch seam allowances for piecing strips and topstitching, and ⅜-inch seam allowances for all other construction.

I originally saw this pattern online and liked it so much that I contacted its creator, Kathy Mack of Pink Chalk Studio (www.pinkchalkstudio.com), who generously allowed me to include it in this book. My favorite part of her design is the continuous topstitching that creates the pencil pockets and gives the piece its structure. It's an elegant finishing solution; and, even better, it's easy and fast. Thank you, Kathy!

1. Prepare Fabric
Wash, dry, and press all fabric.

2. Cut Colored Strips
Arrange the colored prints in order, 1 through 24, from black and brown tones to red, orange, yellow, green, blue, violet, and white and gray tones. Cut one 1⅝-inch x 11-inch strip from the first and last fabrics. Cut the remaining prints into twenty-two 1½-inch x 11-inch strips.

3. Make Interior Pieced Section
Chain-piece (see page 143) the long sides of strips 1 to 2, 3 to 4, 5 to 6, and so on until you've joined all 24 strips into pairs. Trim all the thread tails, and press the seams to the side of the darker fabric.

Sew the neighboring pairs of strips together, stitching strip 1-2 to strip 3-4, strip 5-6 to strip 7-8, and so on until you've joined all strips to make one continuous piece of fabric.

Square up the finished piece (see page 139) by trimming the edges that run perpendicular to the seams, so it measures 10 inches x 24¾ inches. Set the pieced fabric aside.

4. Make Pocket
Cut one 4½-inch x 24¾-inch piece from the pocket fabric and from the pocket-lining fabric. With right sides together and the edges aligned, sew the pocket to the pocket lining along the top edge only. Press the seam open.

Fold the pocket and lining with wrong sides together, and topstitch ¼ inch from the seamed edge.

5. Make Exterior
Cut a 10-inch x 24¾-inch piece from the exterior fabric.

To make and attach the ties, cut the twill tape or ribbon into two 18-inch lengths. Stack the lengths on top of one another, and center the cut ends halfway down the exterior fabric's 10-inch right edge (the tape's or ribbon's long ends should lie across the exterior fabric, and the cut ends should come just past the fabric's edge). Using a zigzag stitch to provide strength, sew the ties within ¼ inch of the exterior fabric's edge.

6. Assemble Pencil Roll
Cut a 10-inch x 24¾-inch piece of flannel for batting. Align and layer the pieces in the following order, from bottom to top: flannel batting; interior pieced section, right side up; pocket, right side up (align unfinished edge with bottom edge of pieced section); exterior fabric, wrong side up. Pin the sides of the layers together.

Using a walking foot on your machine, sew around the roll's four sides, beginning and ending at the top center and leaving a 6-inch opening at top center for turning the piece right side out. Be careful not to catch the ties in your seam.

Trim the corners, and turn the roll right side out. Blindstitch (see page 144) the opening closed by hand.

7. Create Pockets
Using a *hera* marker, mark the pocket seams on the right side of the pocket fabric at 1-inch intervals corresponding to the seams of the interior pieced section. To sew cleanly, set your machine to the needle-down position (if your machine cannot be set this way, hand-turn the machine's fly-wheel to move your needle into the down position before turning the corners as you're topstitching).

Using a walking foot on your machine, sew a straight line from the lower corner of the pocket on the roll's left edge to the upper corner of the pieced section, stopping ¼ inch from the top edge. With needle down, lift presser foot, turn the piece 90 degrees counterclockwise, lower presser foot; then stitch across the roll's upper edge to the first pieced seam (see the stitching diagram at right).

This pencil roll is a great gift for young artists who need to transport their colored pencils back and forth to school. It also makes a good straight-knitting-needle case if you adapt its length to accommodate the longest needles you have (usually 14 inches).

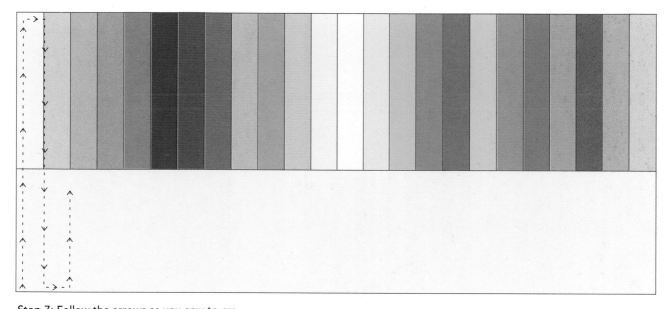

Step 7: Follow the arrows as you sew to create the pencil pockets and give your piece some structure; stitch the pocket seams and stitch-in-the-ditch along the pieced seams, as indicated above. When turning corners, lift presser foot with needle in the down position and rotate fabric 90 degrees.

With the needle down again, lift presser foot, turn the piece 90 degrees counterclockwise, lower presser foot, and stitch-in-the-ditch (see page 148) along the first pieced seam, stopping ¼ inch from the bottom of the roll. With the needle down, lift presser foot, turn the piece 90 degrees clockwise, lower presser foot, sew over to the next crease/pieced seam, stop; and, with the needle down again, lift presser foot, turn the piece another 90 degrees clockwise, lower presser foot and stitch-in-the-ditch up the next pieced seam to the top of the roll. Continue sewing in this fashion until you reach the opposite end of the roll. This single, continuous line of stitching will create individual pencil pockets and provide the roll with structure and strength.

4- to 8-hour gifts

puzzle ball

This project is based on a vintage piece that I picked up in Lancaster County, Pennsylvania, several years ago. With a little research, I found out that it's called a puzzle ball. I smiled when I heard the name because my first few attempts at copying it turned out square! I didn't want to take the original apart to figure out the pattern because I could see that someone had very lovingly hand-stitched the entire thing. One night, after thinking about it off and on throughout the day, the pattern came to me in a flash. I realized that the whole shape was made entirely out of circles! I dashed into my sewing room, where I just had to try it out. Well, it worked, and here it is, albeit slightly more refined.

FINISHED MEASUREMENTS
Approximately 5 inches in diameter

MATERIALS
¼ yard dark, 45-inch-wide, patterned cotton, for main fabric

Three 6-inch squares of light, patterned cotton fabrics

Cotton thread to match dark fabric

Pearl cotton embroidery thread to contrast with fabric (I used bright red)

5½-inch-diameter circle template

Fabric scissors

Hand-sewing needle

Embroidery needle

Twenty-four 1-inch safety pins

Natural cotton stuffing

CONSTRUCTION NOTES
Use ¼-inch seam allowances throughout.

1. Prepare Fabric
Wash, dry, and press the fabric.

2. Cut Fabric
DARK FABRIC
Fold the fabric selvage to selvage, right sides together. Using a pencil and the circle template, trace three circles on the folded fabric. Pin the fabric layers together, and cut around the marked shapes. You will have six circles.

Fold each circle in half, press the fold, and cut along the pressed line to make twelve half-circles. Set them aside.

LIGHT FABRICS
Using a pencil and circle template, trace a circle on the back of one of the light-colored cottons. Cut around the shape. Repeat the process on the other two light fabrics to make three circles in all.

Fold one circle in half twice, carefully aligning the edges, and press the folds. Using a pencil and circle template, draw an arc between the corners of the folded piece to form a pointed ellipse (see the photo on page 56). Pin the layers together, and cut along the line to yield four pointed ellipses. Repeat the process on the other two light fabric circles to make twelve pointed ellipses.

3. Sew Puzzle Pieces
To construct this puzzle ball, you'll make twelve stuffed, quarter-circle segments with dark fabric on two sides and light fabric on the top. Then you'll sew the quarter-circles together at their points to create the ball.

Steps 2-6: Cut the dark fabric into half-circles and the lighter fabrics into pointed ellipses (A). After sewing the ellipses to the half-circles, turn the piece right side out. Stuff and assemble the pieces (B), and then pin and sew the ellipse points together (C).

Place one ellipse on one half-circle, right sides together, so that the top point of the ellipse is at the top of the half-circle and the bottom point of the ellipse falls halfway down the curve of the half-circle. Pin the two fabrics in place along the curved edge, and sew them together ¼ inch from the pinned edge. Sew past the points of the ellipse at each end; you don't need to backstitch because you will reinforce the seam when you sew the other half of the ellipse to the half-circle. Be sure to sew smooth curves so that your puzzle ball will be nice and round.

Take the half-circle you just attached to one side of the ellipse and fold it in half, right sides together; and pin the unsewn edge of the ellipse along the unsewn curved edge of the half-circle. Sew the two edges together from point to point, ¼ inch from the pinned edge. Your seam for this half should just cross the previous seam, ¼ inch from each point.

Sew a seam ¼ inch from the dark cotton's folded edge to make the final shape a more precise quarter-circle. Sew a final seam ¼ inch from the open edge of the piece, from the ellipse end to about halfway down that side, leaving an opening for turning the piece right side out and stuffing it. Set the piece aside. Repeat the process above on the remaining eleven half-circles and ellipses to make twelve quarter-circle puzzle pieces.

4. Trim Puzzle Pieces

Because of the contrast between dark and light fabrics, trim off any dark fabric that shows around the edges of the ellipse so it doesn't show through when you turn your pieces right side out. Also trim off any stray dark threads from the puzzle pieces.

5. Stuff Puzzle Pieces

Turn each puzzle piece right side out, and stuff it firmly. Fold the open edges to the inside, and finger-press them into place. Close the opening by hand with an overhand stitch (see page 145) in a matching thread. (You don't need to blindstitch here because you won't see the seam once your ball is put together, and an overhand stitch is much quicker to do). Set puzzle piece aside. (*Note: Don't worry if your piece looks a little wonky. When you put the ball together, you'll find that this pattern is very forgiving.*)

6. Assemble Ball

Pin the puzzle pieces into place with safety pins, as follows: Begin by pinning two pieces together, joining the point of one ellipse to the point of the second ellipse. Place the pins about ½ inch away from the points so that you'll be able to get your fingers between them when you stitch the pieces together. Add and pin the point of the third ellipse to the first two and then add the fourth. Continue joining points, until all twelve pieces are pinned together in a spherical shape.

7. Finish Puzzle Ball

Cut a 14-inch length of embroidery thread. Thread the needle and tie a quilter's knot (see page 149) at the thread's end. Insert needle into dark fabric about ½ inch from the point of the first ellipse and out just to the left of the ellipse point. Pull thread taut to pop the knot inside (see page 150). Draw the needle back out through the dark fabric, just to the right of the point. Insert the needle again to the left of the point and draw it out to the right of the point, pulling the thread taut. Repeat the process on the adjacent piece, bringing the needle left to right around the ellipse point and around again, before pulling the thread taut. Repeat for the neighboring pair of ellipse points in this foursome.

Slip the needle under the thread sewn at two opposing ellipse points. Wrap around the sewn thread three times to secure the points. Repeat for the second set of opposing ellipse points, wrapping the thread three times around the sewn threads to secure the points. Tie another quilter's knot near the end of the thread and pull the knot inside one of the puzzle pieces.

Repeat the above process around the sphere to secure all twelve ellipses at both points.

This ball makes a great gift for a baby. The colors and shapes appeal to their newly developing senses.

happy birthday pillow

FINISHED MEASUREMENTS
Approximately 12 inches x 16 inches

MATERIALS
8½-inch x 11-inch piece of printable cotton, for pillow center (see Sources for Supplies, page 156)

¼ yard of 45-inch-wide patterned cotton, for inner border

½ yard of 45-inch-wide, coordinating solid cotton, for outer border and pillow back

12-inch x 16-inch pillow form

Cotton thread to match solid cotton

Embroidery thread (I used pearl cotton) in colors to match printed text

Hand-embroidery needle

6-inch embroidery hoop

CONSTRUCTION NOTES
Use ¼-inch seam allowances for piecing pillow top and ½-inch seam allowances elsewhere. For hand-embroidery, use a backstitch (see page 142).

A NOTE ON PILLOW SIZES
I don't like an overstuffed pillow, and these directions reflect my taste. The example shown in the photograph was made with a pillow form 1 inch smaller than its case. The standard convention is to use a pillow form 1 inch larger than the pillowcase. You may want to modify sizes in the directions below according to your stuffing preferences.

For this pillow, I printed a friend's baby's name and birth date—each letter and number in one of three different colors—on printable cotton fabric using an inkjet printer. Then I hand-embroidered around the letters and numbers with pearl cotton. This technique can be used to commemorate any joyous occasion, or could also be used to make a special square on a quilt for a new baby.

1. Make Pillow Center
Following the manufacturer's directions, print your desired text on one piece of printable-cotton fabric. Be sure to leave enough room around your design for a ¼-inch seam allowance.

After printing, remove the fabric's backing, and wash the fabric in soapy water. You can wash it in the sink with dish soap and let it air-dry, or machine-wash and tumble it dry. (Note that if you don't wash the fabric, it will scorch when ironed.) Press the dry fabric.

2. Prepare Remaining Fabric
Wash, dry, and press the other fabrics.

3. Cut Fabric
Cut the printed cotton to your desired size (I cut mine to 7½ inches x 10 inches), leaving enough room around the design for a ¼-inch seam allowance. Set the fabric aside.

Fold the patterned cotton selvage to selvage, and cut one 2½-inch-deep strip for the pillow's inner border. Trim off the selvages, cutting as close to them as possible to give the strip its maximum width. Set the strip aside.

Fold the solid cotton selvage to selvage, and cut a 14-inch-deep strip. Trim off the selvages, and carefully trim away just the fold itself to make two 14-inch x 20-inch rectangles. Set one rectangle aside for the pillow back. Cut the remaining rectangle along its 20-inch length into four 2½-inch-wide strips for the outer border. Set these strips aside.

4. Embroider Letters

Use your embroidery hoop to hold the fabric taut, so that your embroidery will be nice and neat. Embroider around each letter using a backstitch (see page 142) and matching thread color.

5. Piece Pillow Front

Begin sewing the inner border of patterned fabric around the printed-fabric pillow center as follows: Lay the pillow center right side up. ★ Place the 2½-inch strip of patterned fabric, right side down, along the pillow center's top edge. Align the top left corners of the two fabrics, allowing the excess strip fabric to run off the pillow center's right edge. Align and pin the pieces together along the top edge, and sew a seam ¼ inch from the pinned edge, stopping at the corner of the pillow center.

Before pressing your seam, cut the excess strip even with the pillow center's right edge. Press the seam to the side of the darker fabric. Turn the patchwork face up, so that the seam you just sewed runs along the left side. Repeat from ★ until you've attached the inner border to all four sides of pillow center.

Attach the outer border of solid cotton to the inner border just as you attached the inner border.

6. Cut Pillow Front and Back

Trim the pieced pillow front to 14 inches x 18 inches, and cut a pillow back from the solid cotton to the same dimensions. *(Note: Both front and back will be 2 inches larger than the pillow form.)*

7. Sew Pillow

Place the pieced pillow front on the pillow back, right sides together with the edges aligned, and pin the two in place.

Sew around three sides, using a ½-inch seam allowance and beginning and ending with a few backstitches. Trim the corners, and turn the pillow right side out.

Fold each unstitched edge of the pillow fabric ½ inch to the wrong side, and press the fold in place with your iron.

8. Stuff Pillow

Stuff the pillow with the pillow form. Using a blindstitch (see page 144), carefully hand-sew the open edge closed, sewing just inside the fold for the most invisible results.

patchwork tablecloth + napkins

All the different indigo prints in my shop look so beautiful together that when it came time to pick just one for this project, I simply couldn't—so I changed my original plan and picked the whole shelf! For the tablecloth, I cut six fabrics into strips of varying widths and sewed them together to create a rich patchwork. Then from the leftovers of each fabric, I made one napkin.

FINISHED MEASUREMENTS
Tablecloth, approximately 78 inches x 64 inches; napkins, 19 inches square (unfolded)

MATERIALS (FOR TABLECLOTH AND SIX NAPKINS)

2½ yards, 45-inch-wide, main fabric, for tablecloth and one napkin

¾ yards each of six 45-inch-wide different fabrics to complement main fabric, for tablecloth and five napkins

Cotton thread to match most fabric

21 yards small (approximately ¼-inch-wide) rickrack to complement all fabrics

CONSTRUCTION NOTES
Use ¼-inch seam allowances throughout.

1. Prepare Fabric

Wash, dry, and press the fabric and rickrack.

2. Cut Fabric

Fold the main fabric selvage to selvage, and cut one 65-inch-deep piece. Trim the selvages, and set the piece aside for half of the tablecloth.

From the remaining folded main fabric and each piece of complementary fabric, cut one 20-inch-deep piece. Trim the selvages, and cut at the fold to create two 20-inch squares. Set one square aside for a napkin. Cut the other square into several strips from 3 inches in length up to 12 inches in length, which will give you more than enough strips to complete the tablecloth. Your aim is to create a range of strips in various lengths, so you'll have an interesting palette to work with to create the patchwork.

3. Piece Tablecloth

Arrange the patchwork strips you've cut into two columns, each 20 inches wide and at least 68 or 70 inches long. As you lay out your strips, be sure that the fabrics do not repeat too regularly. Sew together the adjacent strips in each column along the 20-inch edges, and press the seams to the side of the darker fabric.

Once both columns are sewn together, square up (see page 139) the edges running parallel to the seams so that each column measures 20 inches x 65 inches. Sew the columns together along the 65-inch edge, and then sew one 65-inch edge of the resulting patchwork to the 65-inch edge of the main fabric.

4. Attach Rickrack

I think it's a good plan to start sewing the rickrack onto the napkins first. Doing this is easy once you get the hang of it but can be a little tricky until you do. If you start with the napkins and need to pull the rickrack out and try again, it'll be a little less daunting than starting with the tablecloth. Here's how to attach the rickrack:

Lay one napkin square right side up. Beginning halfway along one side of the square, pin the rickrack to the napkin's right side ½ inch from the edge. Keep pinning until you're ½ inch from the corner; then fold the rickrack 90 degrees downward so that it's parallel to, and ½ inch inside, the next side of the square. Be sure to place a pin at the corner to secure the rickrack, and then continue pinning it along the new side. At each of the following three corners, fold the rickrack 90 degrees and pin it as before; then continue pinning the rickrack all the way around the napkin, until you come to your beginning point. Cut the rickrack to end where the pinned piece begins.

Sew the rickrack to the napkin, stitching in a straight line down the center of the rickrack, backstitching at the beginning and end of the seam. At every corner, make sure that your needle is in the down position before you lift the presser foot; and then turn the napkin 90 degrees, lower the presser foot, and continue stitching to the next corner. Repeat the process until you come to the end.

5. Finish Tablecloth and Napkins

Turn under the raw edge so that only half of the rickrack shows. The corners should fold under relatively easily if you fold the adjacent side first and then the main edge you're folding over it. Press and pin the folded edge into place. Topstitch all the way around, ¼ inch from the edge.

pinwheel duvet cover

I have always loved the pinwheel design but was intimidated by it for a long time because cutting and sewing triangles can be challenging to do well. This pattern demystifies the pinwheel quilt block with a simple technique for making two right-angle triangles at one time from squares of fabric, which means that you don't cut the triangles until after they're sewn. Instructions for the small pillow top shown in the photo are given at the end of the duvet pattern.

FINISHED MEASUREMENTS
Approximately 80 inches x 90 inches (to fit a queen-size duvet)

MATERIALS
2 yards of 45-inch-wide printed cotton

4¾ yards of 108-inch-wide quilter's muslin

2½ yards snap tape

Cotton thread to match muslin

Zipper foot for your machine

CONSTRUCTION NOTES
Use ¼-inch seam allowances for piecing, and ½-inch seam allowances elsewhere.

1. Prepare Materials
Wash, dry, and press the fabric and snap tape.

2. Cut Fabric
PRINTED COTTON
Fold the fabric selvage to selvage, and cut two 30⅞-inch-deep pieces; then cut each piece down to make two 30⅞-inch squares. Set the squares aside for the pinwheel triangles.

QUILTER'S MUSLIN
Fold the fabric selvage to selvage, and cut one 80½-inch-deep piece. Then trim the selvages so that piece measures 80½ inches x 90½ inches. Set the cut fabric aside for the quilt's back.

Cut two 15½-inch-deep strips, selvage to selvage. Trim the selvages so that each strip measures 15½ inches x 80½ inches. Set the cut pieces aside for the top and bottom borders.

Cut two 10½-inch-deep strips, selvage to selvage. Trim the selvages so that each strip measures 10½ inches x 60½ inches. Set the cut strips aside for the side borders.

Cut one 30⅞-inch-deep strip, selvage to selvage. Cut this strip down to two 30⅞-inch squares, and set them aside for pinwheel triangles.

3. Make Pinwheel Triangles
Place one 30⅞-inch muslin square over one printed-cotton 30⅞-inch square, right sides together, and align the edges. With a pencil and ruler, draw a line from the upper left corner to lower right corner of the muslin square. Pin the fabric together along drawn line to prevent shifting. Sew a seam ¼ inch from

each side of drawn line, and cut along the drawn line. Open up your two new squares, and trim any seam allowance that extends beyond the corners. Repeat the above process with the remaining 30⅞-inch squares, until you have four pieced squares. Press the seams of each half of the pinwheel to the side of the printed fabric.

4. Complete Pinwheel

Lay out your pieced squares as shown in the diagram of the pieced center block below. Then lay the top right square over the bottom right square, right sides together and keeping the correct orientation of the printed fabric to form the pinwheel when opened out again. Align and pin the top edge of the two layered squares, and sew them together ¼ inch from the pinned edge. Press the seam to the side of the printed fabric. Then repeat the process to join the top and bottom left squares.

Align and pin together the edges of the right and left halves of the pinwheel, carefully aligning the points at the center. Sew a vertical seam ¼ inch from the pinned edge. Take care not to sew through the point you made when sewing the horizontal seams. Your vertical seam should just intersect the point where the pinwheel points come together. Press the seam to one side.

Steps 4-5: Lay out the four pieced squares from Step 3 to create the center pinwheel block. Sew center block, then add side borders followed by top and bottom borders.

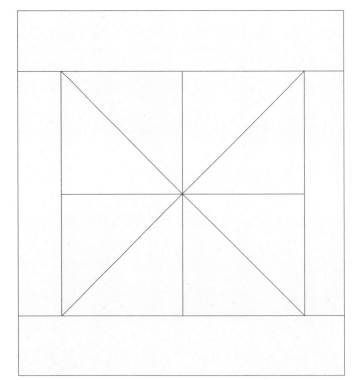

5. Sew Borders to Pinwheel

Fold one 10½-inch x 60½-inch muslin strip carefully in half (making a 10½-inch x 30¼-inch folded strip) to find the exact center. Pin the center of the strip to the center of one side of the pinwheel, right sides together, and then pin the corners of the strip and pinwheel together. Next pin between each pin so that your pins are evenly placed about 2 inches apart down the entire length of the strip. (This method of pinning helps ease out any small errors in your cutting or seam allowances.) Sew the two pieces together ¼ inch from the pinned edge.

Repeat the above process with the remaining 10½-inch x 60½-inch strip on the opposite side of the pinwheel. Pin and sew the top and bottom borders to the pinwheel in the same way.

6. Sew Front and Back Together

Place the pieced pinwheel front on the back fabric, right sides together. Align the fabric edges and corners, and pin around the sides and top of the piece. Sew ½ inch from the pinned edge on three sides, backstitching at the beginning and end of your seam. Turn the duvet right side out.

7. Attach Snap Tape

Attach the zipper foot to your machine. Separate the two layers of snap tape. Pin one length of tape, right side up, to the right side of the pinwheel top, so that the tape just covers the raw edge of the fabric. Position the needle on your machine to the right side of the zipper foot. Sew the tape to the pinwheel top, stitching ⅛ inch from the left edge of the tape.

Repeat this process on the top edge of the quilt back to sew on the remaining side of the snap tape. (It's a good idea to check the position of the pinned tape on the duvet back before sewing it to be sure the snaps meet, adjusting it if need be.)

Fold the partially attached snap tape to the inside of the duvet cover, and pin the unsewn edge in place. Sew the tape ⅛ inch from the pinned edge all the way around the opening of the duvet cover to complete it.

SMALL PILLOW TOP OPTION

To make the 12" pinwheel pillow top, follow directions for creating the pinwheel part of the duvet cover, but cut your fabric squares to 6⅞ inches rather than 30⅞ inches. Follow directions for assembling pillow front and back in the Pieced Pillows pattern on page 37.

Duvet covers make wonderful gifts, and since they don't require any quilting, you can finish them relatively quickly. You could easily adapt any quilt design in this book to be a duvet cover.

peanut, the wee elephant

This charming and lovable elephant, a great gift for children and children at heart, was designed and created by the very talented Hillary Lang of Wee Wonderfuls. I have long admired Hillary's work and am thrilled that she agreed to contribute a pattern to this book. You can find even more great toy patterns, ideas, and inspiration from Hillary at her delightful website www.weewonderfuls.com.

FINISHED MEASUREMENTS
Approximately 7 inches tall x
9 inches long

MATERIALS
½ yard of 45-inch-wide printed cotton fabric, for body

8-inch x 10-inch piece of coordinating cotton, for ear lining

8-inch x 10-inch piece of contrasting cotton, for blanket

Cotton thread to match body fabric

21-inch length of yarn, for braided tail

Small scraps of white and dark-colored wool felt, for eyes

Embroidery thread

Template plastic

Fabric scissors

Sharp tapestry needle

Hand-sewing needle

Natural cotton stuffing or polyfill

Pattern Templates D, E, F, G, H, and I (see pattern sheet page attached to inside back cover of book)

CONSTRUCTION NOTES
Use ¼-inch seam allowances throughout.

1. Prepare Fabric
Wash, dry, and press the fabric.

2. Make Templates
Make **TEMPLATES D, E, F, G, H,** and **I** as well as the two eye pieces (one oval and one circle) from pattern sheet page attached to inside back cover of book. Instead of cutting the templates directly from this book, use template plastic to trace and cut the pieces. Then you'll still have all of the templates in one place, should you ever want to use them again.

3. Cut Fabric
Fold the body fabric selvage to selvage, right sides together. Lay **TEMPLATES D, E,** and **F** on the fabric and trace around them with a pencil. Pin the fabric together, and cut along the marked lines, which will give you two pieces of each shape. Set the cut pieces aside.

Unfold the remainder of the body fabric, and lay it flat, right side down. Place **TEMPLATES G** and **H** on the fabric's wrong side, and trace around them with the pencil. Cut along the marked lines, and set the cut pieces aside.

Fold the ear-lining fabric selvage to selvage, right sides together. Place **TEMPLATE F** on the fabric, and trace around it with pencil. Pin the fabric together, and cut along the marked lines. Set the cut pieces aside.

Fold the blanket fabric selvage to selvage, right sides together. Place **TEMPLATE I** on the fabric, with the marked edge positioned along the fabric's fold and the left edge snug to the folded fabric's left edge, and trace around the template with a pencil. Move the template over to the other edge of the folded fabric, with the marked edge still positioned on the fold, and trace again around the template. Cut along the marked lines. Open up the shapes, and set them aside.

Place the oval-eye template on the white felt scrap, and cut two. Set them aside. Place the circle-eye template on the dark-colored felt scrap, and cut two. Set them aside.

This wee elephant is the perfect size for tiny arms to hug. Try enlarging and shrinking the templates for this project to make a whole family of elephants!

4. Assemble Body
BELLY
Pieces needed: 2 Belly pieces cut from TEMPLATE E
With right sides together, sew together the belly pieces, leaving an opening in the seam, as marked on the template, for stuffing. Press the seam open.

UNDER-TRUNK, BELLY, AND BACK
Pieces needed: Sewn Belly, Under-trunk and Back cut from TEMPLATES G and H
With right sides together, carefully pin the wide end of the Under-trunk (TEMPLATE G) to the Belly front. Next, pin the wide end of the Back (TEMPLATE H) to the Belly back. Sew and press the seams open.

SIDES
Pieces needed: 2 main-fabric Body pieces cut from TEMPLATE D, Sewn Under-trunk, Belly, and Back
With right sides together, carefully pin one side of the body (TEMPLATE D) to the assembled under-trunk, belly, and back. Pin together the leg sections first, and then pin up and around the sides, making sure that the back is on top of piece and the belly on bottom. When everything is matched up correctly and pinned into position, sew and press open the seam. Repeat the process for the other side of the body.

5. Close Trunk
Hand-sew a very loose gathering stitch (see page 145) around the tip of the trunk, about ¼ inch from the edge, to close the trunk. Then pull the thread tight, tie it off, and trim the thread tail.

6. Turn Right Side Out
Clip the seams at the corners to reduce bulk, especially under the legs and along the curve of the trunk. Turn the elephant right side out using the non-hook end of a small crochet hook or a similar tool to help push the trunk and feet outwards. Stuff it firmly. Using a blind-stitch (see page 144), carefully hand-sew the remaining opening closed, stitching just inside the fold for the most invisible results. Set aside.

7. Make Ears
Pieces needed: Two main-fabric ears and two contrasting-fabric ears, cut from TEMPLATE F

Align and pin together one main-fabric ear and one contrasting-fabric ear, right sides together. Sew around the shape, leaving an opening in the seam, as marked on the template. Turn the ear right side out.

Fold under the ear's open edges ¼ inch to the inside, and press the folded edges in place. Blindstitch the opening closed, sewing it together just inside the fold for the most invisible results. Repeat the process for the second ear. Set the assembled ears aside.

8. Make Blanket

Fold under the edges of each of the two blanket pieces ½ inch to the wrong side all the way around, and press the folds in place. Position the two blanket layers wrong sides together, and align and pin the folded edges. Topstitch the blanket ¼ inch from the folded edges, and set it aside.

9. Finish Elephant

ATTACH EARS

Pin the ears to the body where indicated on TEMPLATE D. Hand-sew the straight edge of each ear to the body with a blindstitch, turning over the front corner of each ear ¼ inch, and tacking it into place to create a forward fold in the elephant's ears.

ATTACH BLANKET

Center the blanket over the elephant's back, and tack its corners into place by hand to secure it.

ADD TAIL

Cut three 7-inch-long strands of yarn. Thread all three strands into a tapestry needle, and stitch the yarn through elephant's hind quarters, adjusting the two lengths of yarn to be equal. Separate the yarn into its three two-strand units, and braid them together to the desired length. Tie off the braid with a knot, and trim the yarn ends.

ATTACH EYES

Using embroidery thread, hand-sew the eyes to the elephant's head where indicated on TEMPLATE D.

Hug elephant!

sweet dreams sailboat

I love the old-fashioned 19th-century reproduction fabrics in this quilt. They make the playful design seem a bit more serious. The dark colors give it a peaceful and sleepy feeling. As I made this quilt, I enjoyed seeing what happened to the direction of the prints. I made a point of not planning their direction ahead of time, and I love that some run vertically and some run horizontally. This is a great project to make if you're interested in learning to work with right-angle triangles. It's a lot easier than it looks!

FINISHED MEASUREMENTS
Approximately 44 inches square

MATERIALS
FABRIC 1: 3 yards of 45-inch-wide printed gold cotton, for flag and quilt back

FABRIC 2: 1½ yards of 45-inch-wide printed aqua cotton, for sky

FABRIC 3: ¾ yard of 45-inch-wide printed brown cotton, for boat, mast, and quilt binding

FABRIC 4: ¾ yard of 45-inch-wide printed cream cotton, for sail

FABRIC 5: ½ yard of 45-inch-wide printed dark-aqua cotton, for water

Cotton thread to blend with most fabrics (I used medium taupe)

Natural, thinnest-loft cotton batting, 60 inches x 46 inches

Hera marker

Walking foot for sewing machine

Guide-bar attachment for sewing machine

CONSTRUCTION NOTES
Use ¼-inch seam allowances throughout.

1. Prepare Fabric
Wash, dry, and press the fabric.

2. Cut Fabric
For three of the five fabrics, you'll make a series of cuts. To keep things simple and minimize the need to keep squaring up the cut pieces as you work, you'll make a round of first cuts, then a round of second cuts, and, in two cases, a round of third cuts to each fabric.

FABRIC 1 (QUILT BACK AND FLAG)
For the quilt back, fold the fabric selvage to selvage, and cut two 52-inch-deep pieces. Trim the selvages, and sew the two pieces together along their 52-inch edge. Trim one side so that the final piece measures 52 inches square. Set the piece aside.

For the flag, cut a 4½-inch strip from the fabric left over from the quilt back, Then cut the strip into a 4½-inch square, and set it aside.

FABRIC 2 (SKY)
First Cuts -Fold the fabric selvage to selvage, and cut across the fabric's full width to make:
-Three 6½-inch-deep strips
-One 4½-inch-deep strip
-One 2½-inch-deep strip
-One 19½-inch-deep strip

Second Cuts
-Cut two 6½-inch-deep strips down to 31½ inches wide, and set aside.
-On the third 6½-inch-deep strip, trim the selvages closely so the strip measures 44½ inches wide. If your fabric shrank to less than this width when washed, cut a fourth 6½-inch-deep strip, sew the two 6½-inch-deep strips together, and then cut the resulting piece to 44½ inches wide. *(Note: You can*

use a scrap to add to your strip's length, since the seam does not have to be in the center.) Set aside.

-Cut the 4½-inch-deep strip down to 19½ inches wide, and set aside.

-Cut the 2½-inch-deep strip into one 19½-inch-wide piece and one 12½-inch-wide piece. Set aside.

Third Cuts -Cut the 19½-inch-deep strip into four pieces and set aside:

-One 19½-inch square

-One 12½-inch-deep x 23½-inch-wide rectangle

-Two 6½-inch squares

FABRIC 3 (BOAT, MAST, AND BINDING)

First Cuts - Fold the fabric selvage to selvage, and cut across the fabric's full width to make the cuts below. Then trim the selvages, and set them aside.

-For the boat, one 6½-inch-deep strip

-For the mast, one 1½-inch-deep strip

-For the binding, five 2¼-inch-deep strips

Second Cuts

-Cut the boat strip down to 32½ inches wide.

-Cut the mast strip down to 25½ inches wide.

FABRIC 4 (SAIL)

First Cut - Fold the fabric selvage to selvage, and cut across the fabric's width to make:

-One 19½-inch-deep strip

Second Cut

-Carefully trim off the fold to create two 19½-inch-deep pieces.

Third Cuts

-Cut one piece into a 19½-inch square.

-Cut the other piece into a 12½-inch square. Set aside.

FABRIC 5 (WATER)

Fold the fabric selvage to selvage, and cut one 6½-inch-deep strip. Trim the selvages as closely as possible, and set aside. This piece should measure 44½ inches wide. If your fabric shrank to less than this width when washed, cut a second 6½-inch-deep strip, sew the two strips together along their 6½-inch edge, and cut the piece to 44½ inches wide. *(Note: You can use a scrap to add to your strip's length since the seam does not have to be in the center.)*

3. Piece Quilt Top

LEFT SAIL

Step A. Make Left Sail Patch

Pieces needed: FABRIC 2 (SKY), 19½-inch square; FABRIC 4 (SAIL), 19½-inch square

Lay the sail fabric over the sky fabric, right sides together, and align the edges and corners. With a pencil or *hera* marker, mark a diagonal line from the lower left corner to the upper right corner on the sail fabric. Pin and sew the fabrics together on the marked line. Trim the joined fabrics ¼ inch to the right of the seam. Press the seam to the side of the darker fabric.

Step B. Sew Left Sail Patch to Sky Fabric
Pieces needed: Left Sail Patch; FABRIC 2 (SKY), 2½-inch-deep x 19½-inch-wide strip
Lay the Left Sail Patch right side up, with the corner of the sail fabric at the lower right. Place the Fabric 2 strip, wrong side up, along the bottom edge of the Left Sail Patch. Align, pin, and sew the edges of the two fabrics. Press the seam to the side of the darker fabric, and set aside.

RIGHT SAIL
Step A. Make Right Sail Patch
Pieces needed: FABRIC 2 (SKY), 12½-inch-deep x 23½-inch-wide rectangle;
FABRIC 4 (SAIL), 12½-inch square
Lay Fabric 2 right side up, with the rectangle's short edges at the top and bottom. Place Fabric 4 wrong side up, on top of the rectangle, and align the fabrics' bottom edges. With a pencil or *hera* marker, mark a line from the upper left corner to the lower right corner on the back of Fabric 4. Pin and sew the fabrics together along the marked line. Trim the fabric ¼ inch to the right of the seam. Press the seam to the side of the darker fabric.

Step B. Piece Right Sail Patch to Sky Fabric
Pieces needed: Right Sail Patch, FABRIC 2 (SKY), 2½-inch-deep x 12½-inch-wide strip
Lay the Right Sail Patch right side up, with the corner of the sail at lower left. Place Fabric 2 wrong side up, over the bottom edge of the patch, and carefully align the bottom edges. Pin the layers in place, and sew them together along the pinned edge. Press the seam to the side of the darker fabric, and set the piece aside.

FLAG
Step A. Make Flag Patch
Pieces needed: FABRIC 2 (SKY), 4½-inch-deep x 19½-inch-wide strip;
FABRIC 1 (FLAG), 4½-inch square
Lay Fabric 2 right side up, with the strip's short edges at the top and bottom. Place Fabric 1, wrong side up, over the top of the strip, aligning the top edges and corners. With a pencil or *hera* marker, mark a line from the upper left corner to the lower right corner on the back of Fabric 1, and pin and sew the two fabrics together along the marked line. Trim the fabric ¼ inch to the right of the seam. Press the seam to the side of the darker fabric.

Step B. Sew Flag Patch to Left Sail Patch
Pieces needed: Flag Patch, Left Sail Patch
Lay the Left Sail Patch right side up, with the sail fabric running diagonally from the lower left to the upper right and with the 2½-inch sky strip at the bottom of the patch. Place the Flag Patch, wrong side up, on top, aligning the bottom edge of the Flag Patch with the top edge of the Left Sail Patch. Pin the fabrics into place, and sew along the pinned edge. Press the seam to the side of the darker fabric, and set the piece aside.

Follow Step 3 to assemble the Sweet Dreams Sailboat quilt top.

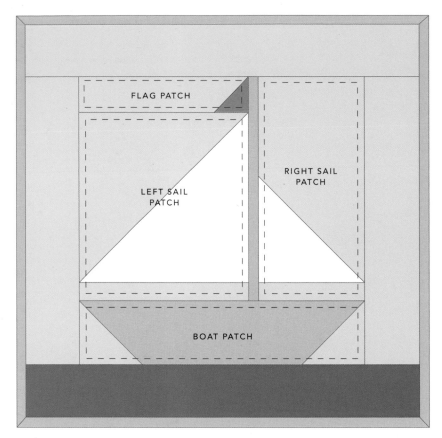

MAST

Step A. Sew Mast to Left Sail Patch

Pieces needed: FABRIC 3 (MAST), 1½-inch-deep x 23½-inch-wide strip; Left Sail Patch

Lay the Left Sail Patch right side up, with the Flag Patch at the top. Place the Fabric 3 strip, wrong side up, over the right edge of the patch. Carefully align the edges and pin them into place. Sew along the pinned edge, and press the seam to the side of the darker fabric.

Step B. Sew Mast to Right Sail Patch

Pieces needed: Left Sail Patch (with mast attached), Right Sail Patch

Lay the Left Sail Patch right side up, with the mast running down the right edge. Place the Right Sail Patch, wrong side up, over the patch's right edge, so the sail bottoms line up. Pin the two edges, and sew them together. Press the seam to the side of the darker fabric.

BOAT

Step A. Make Boat Patch

Pieces needed: FABRIC 2 (SKY), Two 6½-inch squares;

FABRIC 3 (BOAT), 6½-inch-deep x 32½-inch-wide strip

Lay Fabric 3 right side up, with the rectangle's long edges at top and bottom. Place one Fabric 2 square, wrong side up, at each end of the boat fabric, and align the corners and edges. On the left square, mark a diagonal line from the fabric's upper left corner to the lower right corner. Pin the fabric together along the marked line. On the right square, mark a similar line from the lower left corner to the upper right corner, and pin along the marked line. Sew both seams along the marked lines. Trim the outer corners of the piece (away from the center section of the boat) ¼ inch from the seams. Press the seams to the side of the darker fabric.

Step B. Make Sailboat Patch
Pieces needed: Sails, Mast, and Flag Patch; Boat Patch
Lay the Sails, Mast, and Flag Patch right side up, with the flag at top. Place the Boat Patch, wrong side up, on top, so that the boat's top (its longest side) runs along the bottom edge of the other patch. Align the edges; pin and sew the two patches together; and press the seam to the side of the darker fabric.

BORDERS
Step A. Sew Left and Right Sky Strips to Sailboat Patch
Pieces needed: FABRIC 2 (SKY), Two 6½-inch-deep x 23½-inch-wide strips;
Sailboat Patch
Lay the Sailboat Patch right side up, with the boat at the bottom. Place the Fabric 2 strips, wrong sides up, over the right and left sides of the patch. Carefully align the edges, and pin them into place. Sew the strips to the patch, and press the seams to the side of the darker fabric.

Step B. Sew Sky and Water Strips to Sailboat Patch
Pieces needed: FABRIC 2 (SKY), 6½-inch-deep x 44½-inch-wide strip; FABRIC 5 (WATER), 6½-inch-deep x 44½-inch-wide strip; Sailboat Patch (with side borders attached)
Lay the Sailboat Patch right side up, with the boat at the bottom. Place the Fabric 2 strip, wrong side up, over the top edge of the patch. Place the Fabric 5 strip, wrong side up, along the bottom edge of the patch. Carefully align the edges, and pin them in place. Sew the strips to the patch along each pinned edge, and press the seams to the side of the darker fabric.

4. Baste Quilt
Baste the quilt top, batting, and quilt back, following the pin-basting directions on page 147.

5. Machine-Quilt
Attach the walking foot to your machine. Set your guide-bar attachment 1½ inches to the left of the needle (I quilted with horizontal lines 1½ inches apart). Begin in the center, and quilt outwards to the right. Then rotate the quilt 180 degrees, and quilt outwards to the right again.

6. Piece and Attach Binding Strips
Piece the binding strips, following the directions on page 151. Attach the binding, following the directions for the double-fold binding on page 151.

8- to 12-hour gifts

six of one, a half-dozen of the other

This is a great project for beginners because everything about it is simple. The fabric is the real story—it's so bright and colorful that you don't have to do much to it. The quilt is conceived in thirds, with a red peony fabric occupying two-thirds of the front and a third of the back, and a bright red fabric occupying the remaining third of the front and two-thirds of the back. The machine-quilting follows simple, vertical lines approximately 3 inches apart. The name for this quilt came to me when I purchased 6 yards of fabric for the front and 6 yards for the back. Although I didn't end up needing that much fabric to complete the quilt, I liked the name so much I decided to keep it.

FINISHED MEASUREMENTS
Approximately 62 inches x 84 inches

MATERIALS
FABRIC 1: 5 yards of 45-inch-wide floral cotton, for front and back

FABRIC 2: 5 yards of 45-inch-wide patterned cotton, for front and back

FABRIC 3: ¾ yard of 45-inch-wide solid cotton, for binding (I used hot pink)

Large spool of cotton thread to blend with most fabric (I used bright red)

Hera marker

Walking foot for sewing machine

Natural, thinnest-loft cotton batting, 93 inches x 72 inches

CONSTRUCTION NOTES
Use ¼-inch seam allowances throughout.

1. Prepare Fabric
Wash, dry, and press all fabric.

2. Cut Fabric
FABRIC 1
Cut one 84-inch-deep piece. Trim the selvages, so the piece measures 84 inches x 42 inches. Set the piece aside for the quilt front.

Cut one 92-inch-deep piece. Trim the selvages, so the piece measures 92 inches x 20½ inches. Set it aside for the quilt back.

FABRIC 2
Cut one 84-inch-deep piece. Trim the selvages, so the piece measures 84 inches x 20½ inches. Set it aside for the quilt front.

Cut one 92-inch-deep piece. Trim the selvages, so piece measures 92 inches x 42 inches. Set the piece aside for the quilt back.

FABRIC 3
Cut eight 2¼-inch-deep strips, selvage to selvage. Trim the selvages, and set the strips aside for the quilt binding.

3. Piece Quilt Front and Back
To make the quilt front, pin together the 42-inch-wide Fabric 1 piece to the 20½-inch-wide Fabric 2 piece along their 84-inch edges, right sides together. Sew ¼ inch from the pinned edge, and press the seam to the side of the darker fabric. Repeat with the remaining Fabric 1 and Fabric 2 pieces to make the quilt back.

4. Baste Quilt

Arrange the quilt layers as follows: Place the quilt back right side down, with Fabric 1 on the left. Lay the batting on top of the quilt back leaving at least one inch of backing fabric showing all the way around. Place the quilt front over the batting, right side up, with Fabric 1 on the right leaving at least four inches of batting showing all the way around. Pin-baste the quilt, following the directions on page 147.

5. Machine-Quilt

Using the *hera* marker, mark parallel vertical lines for quilting along the quilt front, spacing the lines 3 inches apart. With the walking foot attached to your sewing machine, quilt along the marked lines (for more information on machine-quilting, see page 148). (*Note: If you're running short on time, you can begin by quilting along lines 6 inches apart, and then decide whether you want [or have the time], to quilt between these lines.*)

6. Attach Binding

Piece the binding strips to make one long strip, following directions on page 151. Then attach the binding, following double-fold binding directions on page 151.

just sweet enough

My goal here was to create a quilt that a very feminine little girl would love but wouldn't be sickeningly sweet to adults. I selected six fabrics whose color and style seemed very girly, and then separated them from each other with a lot of white. I used a geometric design but tried not to apply the geometry rigidly. I originally planned to place the colors randomly but felt that the effect was more striking when I arranged the colors to make a spectrum, so I kept them that way. When laying out the shapes, I tried to mix up the sizes in each row but didn't spend too much time worrying over it. The result, I think, is "just sweet enough."

FINISHED MEASUREMENTS
Approximately 60½ inches x 84 inches

MATERIALS
FABRIC 1: 9 yards of 45-inch-wide white cotton, for quilt front, back, and binding

FABRIC 2: ¼ yard each of six 45-inch-wide cotton prints, for piecing (I used polka dots and gingham in a range of pinks and yellows)

Cotton thread to match Fabric 1

Natural, thinnest-loft cotton batting, 93 inches x 72 inches

Hera marker

Walking foot for sewing machine

CONSTRUCTION NOTES
Use ¼-inch seam allowances throughout.

1. Prepare Fabric
Wash, dry, and press all fabric.

2. Cut Fabric
FABRIC 1
Cut two 92½-inch-deep pieces. Trim the selvages, and sew the two pieces together along their 92½-inch edges. Cut the resulting piece down to 68½ inches x 92½ inches, cutting parallel to the seam. Set the piece aside for the quilt back.

Cut the excess fabric left from trimming down the pieced back into five 2¼-inch x 92½-inch strips. Set these strips aside for the double-fold binding.

Fold the remainder of Fabric 1 selvage to selvage, and cut and sew as follows: Cut eighteen 6½-inch-deep strips, and trim the selvages. Pin two strips, right sides together, along their 6½-inch edges; and repeat with the remaining 16 strips to make nine pairs. Sew the pairs together, chain-piecing (see page 143) along their 6½-inch edges. After chain-piecing, carefully snip the threads to separate the pairs, and then press the seams to one side. Cut two of these strips down to 6½ inches x 60½ inches, and set them aside for the top and bottom borders. Cut the remaining seven strips down to 6½ inches x 72½ inches, and set them aside for the sashing and side borders.

Next, cut six 3½-inch-deep strips from Fabric 1, and trim the selvages. Cut each strip into two 8½-inch-wide pieces, two 6½-inch-wide pieces, and two 4½-inch-wide pieces. Set the resulting 36 strips aside for the patches.

From first Fabric 2 piece, cut one 3½-inch-deep strip, selvage to selvage. Trim selvages. Cut this strip into two 8½-inch-wide pieces, two 6½-inch-wide pieces, and two 4½-inch-wide pieces. Repeat with the remaining Fabric 2 pieces. Set the resulting 36 strips aside for the patches.

3. Make Patches

Pin one 8½-inch-wide Fabric 1 piece to one 4½-inch-wide Fabric 2 piece, right sides together, pinning along one of their 3½-inch-deep edges. Continue in the same way, joining each 6½-inch-wide Fabric 1 piece to a 6½-inch-wide

Steps 4-5: Determine the layout of your colored patches, then chain-piece to create six columns. Sew patched columns to background strips, then attach the top and bottom borders.

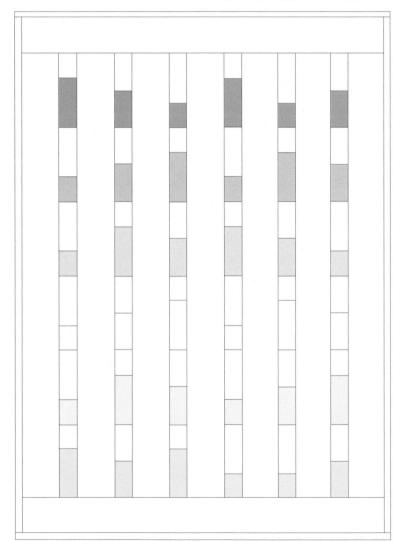

Fabric 2 piece, and each 4½-inch-wide Fabric 1 piece to an 8½-inch-wide Fabric 2 piece. Chain-piece the Fabric 1 and 2 pairs together, for 36 patches total. After chain-piecing, carefully snip the thread between the patches. Press the seams to the side of the darker fabric.

4. Assemble Columns

Arrange the patches as desired into six columns of six patches each. Mark the patches, if necessary, to keep them in order when you chain-piece them. I began by chain-piecing the first and second patch, third and fourth patch, and fifth and sixth patch in each column, and then I pieced these together to form each column. Chain-piece until you've completed all six columns.

5. Assemble Quilt Front

Lay out the quilt with one 6½-inch x 72-inch Fabric 1 strip on both sides of each patched column (see the Patchwork Diagram at left). To join the strips and columns, first fold one Fabric 1 strip and then one column in half to find the exact center of each. Pin the strip to the column at the center point, right sides together, and then pin the ends together. Next pin between the center and end pins, evenly spacing your pins about every 2 inches along the entire fabric. (This method of pinning helps ease out any small errors in your cutting or seam allowances.) Sew the strip to the column along the pinned edge.

Repeat the process above to join the remaining Fabric 1 strips and patched columns. After you've joined all the pairs, you'll have one remaining Fabric 1 strip. Pin and sew this strip to the final pair as you did above. Press all the seams to the patched side. Continue piecing column pairs until they form one rectangle.

Add the top and bottom border strips to the quilt front, using the same method as above to pin out ease before sewing. Sew along the pinned edges, and press the seams to the border side.

6. Baste Quilt

Baste together the quilt front, batting, and quilt back, following the directions for pin-basting on page 147.

7. Machine-Quilt

Attach the walking foot to your machine. Then machine-quilt the layers of fabric together (for more information on machine-quilting, see page 148) in vertical lines that are 3" apart. Using the seams from the patched columns as your guide, pre-mark quilting lines in the Fabric 1 columns and top and bottom borders with your *hera* marker. Stitch-in-the-ditch (see page 148) along the seams of the patched columns and the lines you marked in the borders.

8. Attach Binding

Piece together the Fabric 1 binding strips, following the directions on page 151. Then attach the binding, following the directions for the double-fold binding on page 151

Before assembling your quilt top, try arranging the patches a few different ways to see which way pleases you most.

cutting corners

MATERIALS
FABRIC 1: 1¼ yards of 54-inch-
wide printed floral cotton (or 1½
yards of 45-inch-wide cotton), for
center panel and outer border

FABRIC 2: ¾ yard of 45-inch-wide
patterned cotton, for inner border
(I used dotted cotton)

FABRIC 3: 1¼ yards of 45-inch-
wide solid cotton, for second inner
border

FABRIC 4: ¼ to ⅓ yard of 45-inch-
wide solid cotton, for binding

FABRIC 5: 4 yards of 45-inch-wide
cotton, for quilt back

One large or two small spools of
cotton thread to blend best with all
fabrics (I used light aqua/blue)

One small spool of cotton thread to
match binding fabric

Natural, thinnest-loft cotton batting,
93 inches x 72 inches

1-inch tape maker

Hera marker

Walking foot for sewing machine

CONSTRUCTION NOTES
Use ¼-inch seam allowances
throughout.

I designed this quilt around the fabric I chose for the central panel. Called Mirabelle, it comes from Liberty of London's Tana Lawn line, which is renowned for its beautiful colors and high-quality construction. This fabric's neutral colors, sweet style, and softness make it just right for a baby boy or girl.

Cutting Corners refers to the name of the shortcut technique I used to make the quilt top from long strips of the border fabrics, without measuring their lengths beforehand. The quilting is done in concentric rectangles, which highlights the way the quilt is pieced. To save even more time, I finished this quilt with a machine-attached binding.

1. Prepare Fabric
Wash, dry, and press all fabric.

2. Cut Fabric
FABRIC 1: Cut one rectangle 28½ inches deep x 36½ inches wide, and set it aside for the center panel. Cut five 2½-inch-deep strips, selvage to selvage. Trim the selvages, and set the strips aside for the outer border.

FABRIC 2: Cut four 5½-inch-deep strips, selvage to selvage. Trim the selvages, and set the strips aside for the inner border.

FABRIC 3: Cut six 6½-inch-deep strips, selvage to selvage. Trim the selvages, and set the strips aside for the second inner border.

FABRIC 4: Cut six 1¾-inch-deep strips, selvage to selvage. Trim the selvages, and set the strips aside for the binding.

FABRIC 5: Cut two 70-inch-deep pieces. Trim the selvages.

(Note: In the directions that follow, I've indicated which sides to sew first as you add strips to the quilt front. Be sure to follow these directions, or you may run short on fabric!)

3. Sew Center Panel to Inner Border
Sew one Fabric 2 strip to the Fabric 1 panel along one of its 36½-inch sides.

CUT CORNERS
Before pressing the seam, lay your piece right side up, with the seam running horizontally across the top. Place your ruler over the piece's right edge, across the excess strip, so the ruler's edge is even with the edge of the Fabric 1 rectangle and perpendicular to the seam. Cut the excess strip along the edge of your ruler. Press the seam to the side of the darker fabric.

Repeat the above process with the second Fabric 2 strip, attaching it on the opposite side of the center panel. Your piece now measures 38½ inches x 36½ inches.

Sew the remaining two Fabric 2 strips to the 38½-inch sides of the piece, cutting corners as above. Press the seams to the side of the darker fabric. Your piece now measures 38½ inches x 46½ inches.

4. Add Second Inner Borders
Sew one Fabric 3 strip to each 38½-inch side of the piece, cutting corners as above. Press the seams to the side of the darker fabric. Your piece now measures 38½ inches x 58½ inches.

Sew together two Fabric 3 strips along their 6½-inch edge to make one long strip, and repeat with the remaining two Fabric 3 strips. Sew one of these strips to each 58½-inch side of the center panel. Cut corners, as above, and press the seams toward the darker fabric. Your piece now measures 50½ inches x 58½ inches.

5. Add Outer Border
Sew one Fabric 1 strip to each 58½-inch side of piece. (If you're using 44-inch-wide fabric, you'll have to piece the strips before sewing them, as you did in the previous step.) Cut corners, and press the seams. Your piece now measures 54½ inches x 58½ inches.

Piece together two Fabric 1 strips. Sew the resulting strip to one 54½-inch side of the piece, cutting corners as above. Press the seam to the side of the darker fabric.

Piece together the remaining Fabric 1 strip with the excess fabric from the previous step. Sew the resulting strip to the remaining 54½-inch side of your piece, cutting corners as above. Press the seam to the side of the darker fabric. Your piece now measures 54½ inches x 62½ inches.

6. Assemble Quilt Back
Piece the two Fabric 5 rectangles together along their 70-inch edges. Press the seam to one side. Cut the panel's width from one side to create a piece which measures 70 x 72 inches.

7. Baste Quilt

Baste together the quilt front, batting, and quilt back, following the directions for pin-basting on page 147.

8. Mark Quilt

To prepare for quilting in concentric rectangles, use your *hera* marker to mark the corners of your rectangles. Mark the corners by aligning the ruler with the corners of the pieced fabrics and drawing a diagonal line from each corner to the center of your quilt. (Your lines will not intersect in the center unless you are making a square quilt.) These lines will indicate when to turn the piece 90 degrees as you're quilting.

9. Prepare for Machine Quilting

Attach the walking foot to your machine for quilting, and use the seam guide-bar attachment (see page 136) with the walking foot, setting the guide-bar 1 inch to the left of the needle. Set the machine to the needle-down position. (If your machine cannot be set this way, you'll want to hand-turn the flywheel of your machine to place the needle into the down position before turning corners.) You'll be quilting from the outside border inward to the center panel.

10. Machine-Quilt

FIRST QUILTED LINE: Stitch-in-the-ditch (see page 148) between the outer border (Fabric 1) and the second inner border (Fabric 3). Beginning at one corner of the quilt, sew three or four stitches, backstitch, and sew to the next corner, stopping with your needle in the down position. Lift the presser foot and rotate the quilt 90 degrees, lower the presser foot, and sew to the next corner. Repeat this process until you return to the first corner, and finish with a few backstitches. Remove the quilt from the machine and trim the threads.

BORDERS: Using your guide-bar to maintain 1-inch spacing between the quilt lines, quilt in concentric rectangles, turning the corners as described above, until you reach the center panel.

CENTER PANEL: Set your guide-bar 2 inches to the left of the needle. Quilt the center panel (Fabric 1) as above, but with 2-inch intervals between the quilt lines (this will make the quilting go a little more quickly and make the center panel more supple) until you reach the center of the panel. My smallest quilted rectangle measures 3½ inches x 10½ inches. (*Note: If you're in a big hurry, you can quilt the whole thing with 2-inch spacing between quilt lines, although I would recommend that you also stitch-in-the-ditch between the different fabrics to make your quilt look its best.*)

11. Make Machine-Attached Binding

Piece the Fabric 4 binding strips, following the directions on page 151. Then fold the binding and attach it to the quilt, following the directions for a machine-attached binding on page 152.

little bits

I wanted this quilt to look modern despite being made out of 19th-century reproduction fabrics, and I think it does. I love the quiet, restful feeling of the dark fabric, and the way the blue "little bits" shine out from it.

FINISHED MEASUREMENTS
Approximately 64½ inches x 67 inches

MATERIALS
FABRIC 1: 4¼ yards of 45-inch-wide printed dark cotton, for quilt front and binding

FABRIC 2: ⅛ to ¼ yard (or at least a 1½-inch x 20-inch strip) of six different printed blue cottons, for "little bits"

FABRIC 3: 4¼ yards of 45-inch-wide cotton, for quilt back

Cotton thread to match Fabric 1

Natural, thinnest-loft cotton batting, 93 inches x 72 inches

1-inch tape maker

Hera marker

Walking foot for sewing machine

CONSTRUCTION NOTES
Use ¼-inch seam allowances throughout.

1. Prepare Fabric
Wash, dry, and press all fabric.

2. Cut Fabric
FABRIC 1
Fold the fabric selvage to selvage, and cut three 6½-inch-deep strips across the fabric's width. Trim the selvages; then trim the folds to make six pieces measuring 6½ inches x 20 inches. Set the strips aside for piecing.

With the fabric still folded, cut two 64½-inch-deep pieces, selvage to selvage. Trim the selvages to create two pieces measuring 40 inches wide and 64½ inches deep. Set one aside for the top of the quilt front. Cut the second piece into two pieces measuring 20 inches wide and 64½ inches deep. Set one of these pieces aside for the bottom of the quilt front. Cut the remaining piece into five 1¾-inch-wide x 64½-inch-deep strips. Set these strips aside for the machine-attached binding.

FABRIC 2
Cut a strip 1¾ inches deep and 20 inches wide from one of the six little-bits fabrics. Repeat with the remaining Fabric 2 pieces, and set the cut pieces aside.

FABRIC 3
Fold the fabric selvage to selvage, and cut two 72-inch-deep pieces across the fabric's width. Trim the selvages, and sew the pieces together along their 72-inch edges. Cut down the width of the resulting piece to 74 inches. Set the piece aside for the quilt back. (You can use the excess fabric for one of your little-bits strips in the next step.)

3. Make Little-Bits Panels
Lay one of the 6½-inch x 20-inch Fabric 1 pieces on your cutting mat, right side up and with the 20-inch edge positioned vertically. Using your straight-edge ruler, cut a diagonal line from top to bottom through the fabric's

Diagram A

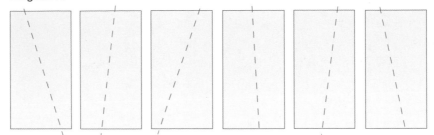

Step 3: Use your rotary cutter and ruler to
make diagonal cuts to Fabric 1 rectangles.

6½-inch edges, cutting at a slight angle to the fabric's 20-inch edge, and starting and ending
the cut at least 1 inch in from the corners. (See Diagram A.)

With right sides together, sew a Fabric 2 strip along one cut edge of the Fabric 1 piece,
and then sew the remaining half of the Fabric 1 piece to the other edge of the Fabric 2 strip,
making a new panel with a colored strip running through it at an angle. Press the seams to
the side of the darker fabric. Repeat the process above using different angles to cut the
remaining Fabric 1 pieces and join them to the remaining Fabric 2 strips, creating a total of
six panels. (See Diagram B.)

Diagram B

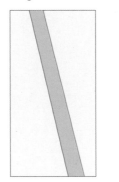

Step 3: Inset Fabric 2 strips.

Diagram C

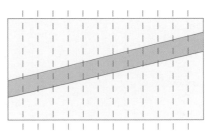

Step 4: Cut inset rectangles into
1½-inch little-bits strips.

4. Cut Little-Bits Strips
Cut each panel into 1½-inch-wide strips, cutting perpendicular to the 20-inch edge. You should
get approximately 12 or 13 little-bits strips from each panel. (See Diagram C.)

5. Assemble Little-Bits Block
Arrange 64 little-bits strips, with their 6½-inch edges together, into one long row that seems
harmonious (you will have some leftover strips). (See Diagram D.)

Diagram D

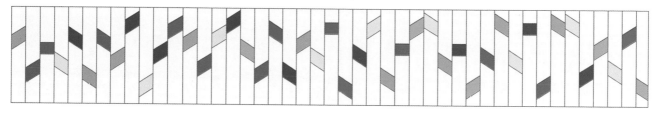

Step 5: Arrange 64 little-bits strips
as desired and piece together.

Chain-piece (see page 143) the strips into pairs, sewing along the 6½-inch edges as follows:
Piece Strip 1 to Strip 2, Strip 3 to Strip 4, Strip 5 to Strip 6, and so on, ending by piecing Strip
63 to Strip 64.

Next, chain-piece the pairs of strips as follows: Piece Strips 1-2 to Strips 3-4, Strips 5-6 to Strips
7-8, Strips 9-10 to Strips 11-12, and so on, ending by piecing Strips 61-62 to Strips 63-64.

Continue chain-piecing strips in this way until you've sewn together all 64 strips into one
6½-inch x 64½-inch block.

6. Piece Quilt Front
Sew one 64½-inch x 40-inch Fabric 1 piece to the top of your block. Sew the other 64½-inch
x 20-inch Fabric 1 piece to the bottom of your block. Press the seams away from the block.
(Note: Because of all its seams, the little-bits block is extremely elastic. When you sew it to
the other pieces of your quilt top, I recommend that you use lots of pins to secure the layers
and also that you sew with the walking foot on your machine to prevent the block from
stretching as you sew.)

7. Baste Quilt
Baste the quilt front, batting, and quilt back, following the directions for pin-basting on
page 147.

8. Mark and Quilt
Use your hera marker to mark your quilting lines. I marked my quilting lines 1 inch apart to
correspond with the seams on the little-bits block. Machine-quilt along the marked lines,
following the directions for machine-quilting on page 148.

9. Piece and Attach Binding
Piece together the Fabric 1 binding strips, following the directions on page 151. Then attach
the binding, following the directions for making a machine-attached binding on page 152.

summer breeze

I call this quilt Summer Breeze because of its sunny, summery colors, and because it's so easy to make. It's the perfect casual quilt to take out for a catnap on a summer day or a picnic in the grass, which makes it a wonderful gift for a family that has a summer home with a big green lawn. Instead of being quilted, this project is held together with ties, which is the way my grandmother Cordelia always finished her quilts. The 1930s reproduction feed-sack fabrics are sweet, pretty, and friendly, just like her.

FINISHED MEASUREMENTS
Approximately 60 inches x
81 inches

MATERIALS
FABRIC 1: 8 yards of 45-inch-wide printed cotton, for quilt front, back, and binding

FABRIC 2, 3, 4, AND 5: ¾ yard each of four 45-inch-wide cotton prints, for piecing

Cotton thread to blend best with all five fabrics (I used pale green)

Natural, thinnest-loft cotton batting, 93 inches x 72 inches

One skein of wool yarn, for quilt ties

Sharp tapestry needle (with smallest eye your yarn will fit through)

CONSTRUCTION NOTES
Use ¼-inch seam allowances throughout.

1. Prepare Fabric
Wash, dry, and press all fabrics.

2. Cut Fabric
FABRIC 1
Horizontal Strips
Fold the fabric selvage to selvage, and cut four horizontal strips across the fabric's folded width, as follows: one 12½-inch-deep strip, one 6½-inch-deep strip, one 4½-inch-deep strip, and one 2½-inch-deep strip. Trim all selvages, and set the strips aside.

Vertical Strips
With the fabric still folded, cut one 82-inch-deep piece. Then fold the cut piece once more in half, aligning the fold and the selvages. Trim the fold and selvages to cut a 10½-inch-wide strip. You will now have four 82-inch-deep x 10½-inch-wide strips.

Quilt Back
Cut two 88-inch-deep pieces. Trim the selvages, and cut 10¾ inches off the width of each piece. Align, pin, and sew the two resulting 34¼-inch-wide pieces together along the 88-inch edge to produce an 88-inch-deep x 68-inch-wide rectangle. Set the piece aside for the quilt back.

Binding Strips
Using one of the two 10¾-inch-wide x 88-inch-deep panels cut off the pieced quilt back, cut four 2¼-inch-wide x 88-inch-deep strips. This will give you more than enough fabric for binding your quilt.

After making five multicolored panels (Step 2), and cutting the panels into three strips (Step 3), arrange and piece the strips into three 82-inch-long columns, piecing them to the background strips to make the quilt front (Steps 4-5).

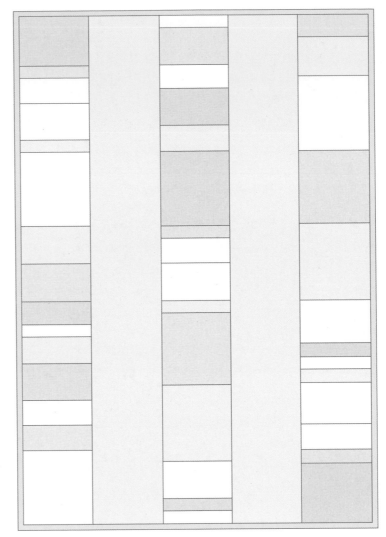

FABRICS 2, 3, 4, AND 5

Cut four horizontal strips from Fabric 2 piece as follows: one 12½-inch-deep strip, one 6½-inch-deep strip, one 4½-inch-deep strip, and one 2½-inch-deep strip. Trim all selvages, and set the strips aside. Repeat with Fabrics 3, 4, and 5, for 16 horizontal strips.

2. Piece Multicolored Panels

Separate the horizontal strips into five groups, with one piece of each fabric in each group. Vary the sizes of the strips in each group as much as possible. Sew each group along the long edges to form five multicolored panels. Press the seams to the side of the darker fabric.

3. Cut Multicolored Strips

After you've sewn the five panels, cut each into three 12½-inch-wide vertical strips. Begin by squaring up (see page 139) the edge perpendicular to your seams, and cut three 12½-inch-wide strips, measuring in from that edge. When all panels are cut, you will have 15 multicolored strips. A helpful hint: If you're space-challenged, as I am living in New York City, it helps to fold your fabric first, right sides together, along one of the central seams, so that you can cut the vertical pieces using a 24½-inch ruler.

4. Piece Multicolored Columns

Arrange the strips into three multicolored columns that are approximately 90 inches long each (and no shorter than 82 inches long). Vary the order of your strips so that the colors do not repeat too regularly; you may need to trim the end off some strips in order to separate the colors. Keep in mind that the resulting columns will be separated from each other by a 10½-inch-wide strip of Fabric 1. Before sewing, place one safety pin at the top of the first column, two at the top of the second, and three at the top of the third, to help you keep track of your overall design. Sew together the strips along the 12½-inch edges to form three columns at least 82 inches long.

5. Piece Quilt Front

You may find that some of the multicolored columns are longer than the vertical Fabric 1 strips. Before joining the columns to the Fabric 1 strips, decide which end of these columns should be trimmed, so that each column is the same length as the Fabric 1 strips (82 inches), and trim accordingly. Next, pin and sew the three multicolored columns along their 82-inch edges, with the two Fabric 1 strips inbetween them. Press the seams to the side of the darker color. Square up the top and bottom edges, so that the quilt front measures approximately 60 inches x 81 inches.

6. Baste Quilt

Baste the quilt front, batting, and quilt back together, following the directions for pin-basting on page 147.

7. Tie Quilt

Using yarn, tie the quilt at regular intervals, following the directions for tying a quilt on page 150. I placed my ties 4 inches apart.

8. Attach Binding

Piece binding strips, following the directions on page 151. Attach the binding, following the directions for the double-fold binding on page 151.

When making the five multicolored panels in Step 2, mix up the colors and sizes of the blocks so you don't repeat your arrangement from panel to panel.

stacked coins

FINISHED MEASUREMENTS
Approximately 52½ inches x
65½ inches

MATERIALS
FABRIC 1: 3 yards of 45-inch-wide
solid cotton, for quilt front

FABRIC 2: ¼ yard each of eight
or more 45-inch-wide cottons, for
"coins" (scraps are good too, but
need to be at least 20 inches wide)

FABRIC 3: 4¼ yards of 45-inch-
wide cotton, for quilt back

FABRIC 4: ½ yard of 45-inch-
wide cotton, for binding

Cotton thread to blend with
Fabric 2, for piecing (I used
medium taupe)

Cotton thread to contrast with
Fabric 1, for machine quilting
(I used bright orange)

Natural, thinnest-loft cotton batting,
93 inches x 72 inches

Walking foot for sewing machine

Hera marker

CONSTRUCTION NOTES
Use ¼-inch seam allowances
throughout.

I've always loved the whimsical charm of vintage stacked-coin quilts (also known as Chinese coin quilts), which were typically made with solid fabrics as crib quilts in Amish communities. Some reading on the subject suggests that the design is a reinterpretation of the more formal Amish bars quilts. This version uses printed fabrics for the "coins" to accentuate the feeling of movement in the design. Because the coins are made of irregularly shaped pieces, it's the perfect opportunity to use fabric scraps from your stash or remnants cut from someone's childhood clothes, making a very special gift.

1. Prepare Fabric
Wash, dry, and press all fabric.

2. Cut Fabric
FABRIC 1
For the quilt front's top and bottom borders, fold the fabric selvage to selvage, and cut one 52½-inch-deep piece. Trim the selvages and the fold, and cut the piece down to make two 52½-inch-deep x 10½-inch-wide rectangles. Set them aside.

For the quilt front's side borders and sashing (the background between columns), cut one 46-inch-deep piece from the remaining folded fabric, and trim the selvages. Cut two 10½-inch-wide strips running the length of this piece, and then four 3½-inch-wide strips running the length of this piece. Set the strips aside.

Use the remainder of Fabric 1 for coin strips, if desired. (I made 16 coin strips from this fabric, positioning them in different places in each column to variously break up the colored coins.)

FABRIC 2
Start making the coin strips by folding one Fabric 2 piece selvage to selvage. Trim the selvages and trim the fold, to make two rectangles measuring 9 inches deep x 20 inches wide. Cut each rectangle into strips along the 20-inch

width, cutting freehand (without your ruler). Make the strips a range of depths, from about 1 inch to 4 inches. Repeat the process with the remaining Fabric 2 pieces, which will give you more than enough strips to work with.

FABRIC 3

From Fabric 3, cut two 74-inch-deep pieces for the quilt back. Trim the selvages, and sew the two pieces together along their 74-inch edge. Cut the resulting piece down parallel to the seam to measure approximately 61 inches x 74 inches, and set it aside for the quilt back. Use the remainder of Fabric 3 for coin strips, if desired.

FABRIC 4

From Fabric 4, cut seven 2¼-inch-deep strips. Trim the selvages and set them aside for the binding. Use the remainder of Fabric 4 for coin strips, if desired.

2. Sew Coin Strips into Panels

Arrange the coin strips into panels, with one of each Fabric 2 strip per panel plus strips from the remnants of Fabrics 1, 3, and 4, if desired. Mix up the colors and sizes of the strips as you work to avoid repeating them too regularly from panel to panel. Pin and sew the strips together along the 20-inch edges, stitching ¼ inch from the pinned edge and pressing the seams to the side of the darker fabric. You should aim to have about six or seven panels.

3. Cut Panels into Coin Patches

Square up (see page 139) the panel edges along the shorter sides. Cut each panel into four 4½-inch-wide strips, cutting perpendicular to your seams.

4. Sew Patches into Columns

Arrange the coin patches into five columns, at least 46 inches long each. Once you're satisfied with your design, square up the patches along their 4½-inch edges so that they'll make straight columns when you piece them together. To square them up, lay the first two patches in a column both facing right side up, one above the other, with their 4½-inch edges touching. Decide where you want to position the horizontal seam that will join the two patches. Then overlap just the touching ends of the upper patch and lower patch, so each patch extends ½ inch beyond your desired horizontal seamline (the overlap provides for your ¼-inch seam allowance and a ¼-inch leeway). Cut through both layers of fabric with your rotary cutter along your intended seamline. Repeat the process with the remaining patches at the overlaps.

Mark the patches, if necessary, to ensure that you can keep them in order when you chain-piece (see page 143) them together into columns. I began by chain-piecing the first and second patch, the third and fourth patch, and the fifth and sixth patch in each column; and then I pieced these pairs together. Chain-piece the patches until all five columns are complete. Press the seams to the side of the darker fabric, and square off the top edge of each column.

5. Piece Quilt Front

Lay out the quilt front right side up, with the 46-inch-deep x 10½-inch-wide Fabric 1 borders outside of the first and last coin columns and the 46-inch-deep x 3½-inch-wide Fabric 1 sashing strips between each column.

Piece the columns to the Fabric 1 strips as follows: Align and pin the first column to the first Fabric 1 side border, right sides together and beginning at the top of each piece. Sew the column and border together ¼ inch from the pinned edge. Press the seam to the side of the darker fabric. Next align and pin the other long side of the same column to a Fabric 1 sashing strip, and sew the two together ¼ inch from the pinned edge. Continue sewing the remaining columns and strips together, working your way across the quilt front and ending with the second Fabric 1 side border. Once you've sewn together all the columns, sashing pieces, and side borders, square off the bottom edge of the piece (you may have to cut it a little shorter than 46 inches to make it square).

Pin the remaining Fabric 1 top and bottom border strips to the quilt front, right sides together. Sew each seam ¼ inch from the pinned edge, and press the seams to the border side.

6. Baste Quilt

Pin-baste the quilt, following the directions on page 147.

7. Machine-Quilt

Attach the walking foot to your machine, and quilt the basted layers together in your desired pattern. I quilted mine in a diamond pattern that I made by marking intersecting diagonal lines every 4 inches across the quilt front with a *hera* marker.

8. Attach Binding

Piece binding strips, following the directions on page 151. Then attach the binding, following the directions for the double-fold binding on page 151.

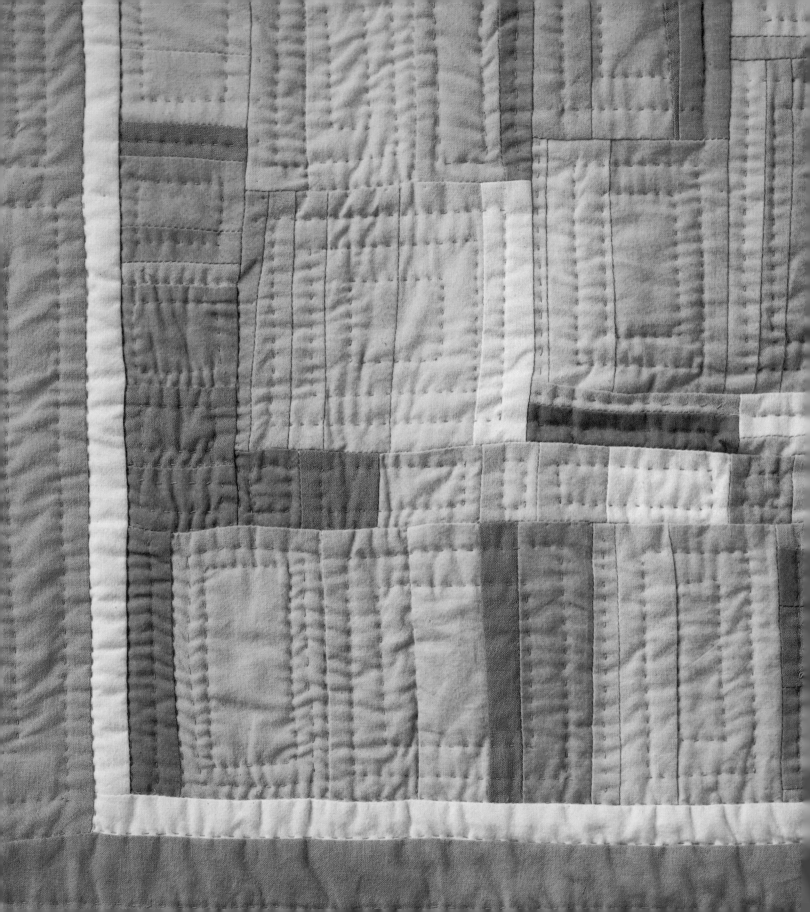

more-than-12-hour gifts

follow-the-lines baby quilt

This quilt is very simple to make, but the hand-quilting does take some time. The story here is the joyfulness of the fabric, which lends itself especially well to being quilted along the lines because it includes both large and small designs. Cassandra Thoreson, who teaches at Purl Patchwork, made this quilt for me. We selected bright red for the hand-quilting thread and the binding to accentuate the playfulness of the fabric.

FINISHED MEASUREMENTS
Approximately 34 inches x
40 inches

MATERIALS
FABRIC 1: 1 yard of 45-inch-wide printed cotton (with a design that varies in size), for quilt front

FABRIC 2: 1¼ yards of 45-inch-wide, coordinating printed cotton, for quilt back

FABRIC 3: ½ yard of 45-inch-wide solid cotton, for binding

Hand-quilting thread

Hand-quilting needle(s)
(I prefer size 10 betweens)

Wool batting, 36 inches x 46 inches
(*Note: If you use Quilter's Dream wool or cotton batting, your stitching can be up to 8 inches apart and the batting will remain stable. If you use another brand, be sure to check the manufacturer's directions for the maximum distance between stitches.*)

1. Prepare Fabric
Wash, dry, and press all fabric.

2. Cut Fabric
FABRIC 1
Square up (see page 139) the sides of the fabric, and trim the selvages. You should be left with a piece that is approximately 34 inches x 40 inches, but no larger than the depth or width of the batting (36 inches x 46 inches).

FABRIC 2
Square up sides of the fabric, and carefully trim the selvages. You should be left with a piece that is approximately 43 inches x 41 inches.

FABRIC 3
Fold the fabric selvage to selvage, cut five 2¼-inch-deep strips, and trim off the selvages. Set aside for binding.

3. Baste Quilt
Thread-baste the quilt front, batting, and quilt back (see page 147).

4. Quilt by Hand
Following the lines of the print, begin hand-quilting the outlines of the large designs all over the quilt. (For more information on hand-quilting techniques, see page 149.) Stitch around the medium-sized designs next, and then the smaller designs. If you work across the entire quilt continuously, rather than focusing on one part at a time, you can decide that it's done when it looks right. You'll also avoid being locked into a really dense design from the beginning.

5. Attach Binding
Piece binding strips, following the directions on page 151. Attach the binding, following the directions for the double-fold binding on page 151.

color-wheel quilt

MATERIALS

FABRIC 1: 7¼ yards of 45-inch-wide white cotton, for background, binding, and quilt back

FABRIC 2: 52 different-color printed cottons, at least 4 inches x 12 inches each (*Note: When picking out your colors, it's helpful to divide them into four quadrants of 13 colors each. [This is also how you'll construct the color wheel.] Here's how I organized my quadrants:*
1. Magenta to pink-orange
2. Orange to yellow
3. Yellow-green to blue-green
4. Blue to purple)

Cotton thread to blend best with all colors, for piecing (I used light grey)

Large spool (about 273 yards) of cotton thread, for quilting (I used light taupe)

Natural, thinnest-loft cotton batting, 93 inches x 72 inches

Heavy-duty template plastic

Pattern paper

Pattern templates L, M, and N (see pattern sheet page attached to inside back cover of book)

Hera marker

Walking foot for sewing machine

CONSTRUCTION NOTES
Use ¼-inch seam allowances throughout.

This quilt is really simple to make. The biggest challenge (and the most exciting part) is picking out the fabric! Scraps and fat quarters are a great resource for this quilt, in which you'll want your colors to fall into some sort of spectrum. Don't worry if your colors seem imperfect in their flow; once the quilt is all together, you'll be amazed by how well it works. In fact, I think it's nice for a few colors to stand out from the progression around the color wheel—it adds sparkle to the quilt.

1. Prepare Fabric
Wash, dry, and press all fabric. This is especially important if you're using any vintage or hand-dyed fabrics that may bleed when you wash them. You don't want any dye bleeding onto the white background when you wash your quilt.

2. Make Templates
Make **TEMPLATES L, M,** and **N** from pattern sheet page attached to inside back cover of book. Instead of cutting the templates directly out of this book, trace the large pieces using pattern paper and the small piece using template plastic; then cut the templates from those materials. That way you'll still have all of the templates in one place, should you ever want to use them again.

3. Cut Fabric
FABRIC 1
First Cuts
-Fold the fabric selvage to selvage, and cut one 12-inch-deep strip across the fabric's width. Set the strip aside for the center circle, and leave the rest of the fabric folded.
-Cut four 25-inch-deep strips, selvage to selvage (you'll trim off the selvages later). Set the strips aside for the outside arcs, and leave the rest of the fabric folded.
-Cut seven 2¼-inch-deep strips, selvage to selvage. Trim the selvages. Set the strips aside for the binding, and leave the rest of the fabric folded.
-Cut two 62-inch-deep pieces. Trim the selvages. Sew these two strips together along their 62-inch edge, and cut the pieced fabric's width down to 62 inches. Set the pieced square aside for the quilt back.

Second Cuts

MAKE QUARTER-CIRCLES AND OUTER ARCS

Fold the 12-inch-deep Fabric 1 strip again, aligning the fold and selvages. Pin TEMPLATE L to the fabric, aligning the fabric's straight grain (its length) with the marked grain line on the template. Trace and cut around the template, to make four quarter-circles, and set aside.

Lay one 25-inch-deep Fabric 1 strip on top of a second 25-inch-deep strip, aligning the folds and edges of the two pieces. Pin TEMPLATE M to the layered fabric, placing the edge noted on the template along the fabric's fold. Trace and cut around the template to make two outer arcs. Repeat the process with the remaining two 25-inch-deep strips. Finger-press the center fold of each outer arc, and set them aside.

4. Organize Color-Wheel Fabrics

Organize your Fabric 2 prints into four groups of 13 colors each, making sure that each quadrant leads nicely into the next, and that the colors within each quadrant flow together well.

5. Assemble Color-Wheel Quadrants

CUT COLOR-WHEEL FABRIC

You can cut three or four colors at once by stacking them on top of one another, wrong side up and with the edges aligned. On the back of the top fabric, use a pencil to trace around TEMPLATE N. With your straight-edge ruler and rotary cutter, cut along the drawn lines. Continue cutting until you've cut all 13 colors for your quadrant.

Before sewing the quadrant, check to see how the colors look together to be sure that you like their order (I made a few changes once I saw them laid out in an arc). After deciding on your design, pencil-mark the pieces lightly on the back in order from 1 to 13 before piecing them.

MAKE COLORED ARC

Align and chain-piece (see page 143) the neighboring pairs of colored strips along their long edges. After clipping the threads between the sewn pairs, press the seams to the side of the darker fabric. Chain-piece the neighboring joined pairs in order again, continuing until you've joined all 13 pieces of the color arc. It's worth checking (and re-checking) to see that your strips are in order as you sew them; with so many similar colors, it's easy to mix them up.

MAKE QUADRANT

Fold the colored arc in half, finger-pressing the center fold. Align the center of arc with the center fold line of one outer background arc (TEMPLATE M), and pin the pieces together at their centers, right sides together. Then pin the pieces at each end, and continue pinning between the pins until there is about 1 inch between each pin. Sew ¼ inch from the pinned edge to join the two pieces, stitching carefully in a smooth line, so your curve will be nice and rounded. Press the seam to the side of the colored fabric.

Complete the quadrant by sewing the colored arc to the quarter-circle (**TEMPLATE L**), folding and pinning in a similar fashion as above. Press the seam to the side of the colored fabric. Set the quadrant aside.

Repeat this entire step to make the remaining three quadrants of the quilt front. Be sure to sew your fabrics in the right order. (It's pretty easy to sew them together in the opposite direction of what you intended!)

6. Assemble Quilt Front
Arrange the quadrants in the desired order, and then sew together the top two quadrants and then the bottom two, right sides together, along their center vertical seam. Press the seam in opposite directions on each sewn half. Complete the quilt front by sewing the horizontal seam (with right sides together) that joins the two halves. Take care to align the color-wheel seams before you sew both seams, and press each seam to one side.

7. Baste Quilt
Baste together the quilt front, batting, and quilt back, following the directions either for pin-basting on page 147 or thread-basting on page 147, according to your preference. (Pin-basting tends to go more quickly than thread-basting, but it's easier to mark your quilting lines if you've thread-basted—and this quilt has a lot of lines to mark.)

8. Mark Quilt
With the *hera* marker and a ruler, mark quilting lines on the quilt front. Use the seams between each color in the wheel as your guide for extending quilt lines onto the white background fabric. It's okay to cheat your lines a little in the center if necessary, so they intersect nicely.

9. Machine-Quilt
Attach the walking foot to your sewing machine, and thread the machine with the quilting thread you plan to use. Quilt along the marked lines, beginning with the seams where you pieced your quadrants together, and then moving clockwise around the quilt. Be sure to begin and end sewing each quilting line beyond the edge of the quilt front to prevent your stitches from pulling out in the future.

Finish quilting by stitching-in-the-ditch (see page 148) around the outside and inside curves of the color wheel, backstitching at the beginning and end of your seam.

10. Piece and Attach Binding
Piece the binding strips, following the directions on page 151. Then attach the binding, following the directions for the double-fold binding on page 151.

Stand back and admire your quilt. It's beautiful!

washed silk quilt

Many years ago, I saw some quilts from Morocco that paired a luxurious silk charmeuse on one side with raw muslin on the other. I found the juxtaposition of the two fabrics both surprising and beautiful. I've often thought of these quilts and am happy to share my version with you. I used a wool batting for this quilt to make it light and lofty as well as machine-washable.

FINISHED MEASUREMENTS
Approximately 52 inches x 70 inches

MATERIALS
FABRIC 1: 2 yards of 54-inch-wide iridescent silk taffeta, for quilt front

FABRIC 2: 5 yards of 42-inch-wide solid cotton, for quilt back and binding

Wool batting, 93 inches X 72 inches

Cotton sewing thread to match Fabric 2

Pearl cotton embroidery thread, about 100 yards (I used bright yellow)

4 embroidery or sashiko needles

18-inch square, lap-size quilting frame

Hera marker

Thimble

CONSTRUCTION NOTES
Use 4 large embroidery or sashiko needles to hand-quilt 4 lines at a time with embroidery thread.

1. Prepare Fabric
Silk taffeta comes with a lot of sizing in it, so it's important to wash it before use to soften it. It can be pretty wrinkled when it comes out of the dryer, but don't be alarmed. After drying, spray with water and press with a hot iron. (I find a cotton setting works well, but be sure to test it out on the edge of your fabric first, to avoid burning.) Wash, dry, and press the fabric for the quilt back as well.

2. Cut Fabric
FABRIC 1
Carefully trim the selvages and square up (see page 139) the sides, so that your piece measures approximately 52 inches x 70 inches. Set the piece aside for the quilt front.

FABRIC 2
Cut two 78-inch-deep pieces. Trim the selvages, align the pieces right sides together, and sew them along their 78-inch edge. Cut the pieced fabric down to 60 inches, and set it aside for the quilt back. From the excess fabric left from trimming down the pieced back, cut seven 2¼-inch-wide strips along the 78-inch side. Set the strips aside for the quilt binding.

3. Baste Quilt
Thread-baste the quilt front, batting, and quilt back, following the directions for thread-basting on page 147. The wool batting and silk can both be very slippery to work with, so it's important to thread-baste the quilt very well. I made my basting lines 2 inches apart, rather than the usual 3 inches.

4. Hand-Quilt
Using the *hera* marker, mark parallel vertical lines 1½ inches apart on the quilt front. Position your 18-inch-square lap-quilting frame on the quilt so that you can hand-quilt four partial lines, using a different needle for each line, before moving the frame (this will help you get your quilting done more quickly).

The simplicity of this project makes it the perfect gift for almost anyone. It would fit beautifully in a home with a modern or eclectic sensibility, and could even become a child's favorite blanket.

Thread each needle with a 20-inch length of embroidery thread, and quilt each line with its own needle as follows before moving the frame down the quilt:

Tie a quilter's knot (see page 149) at each thread end. Beginning at the top of the quilt, insert the needle into the quilt front and draw it back out again at the beginning of your quilting line, popping the knot to the inside of the quilt. Quilt with a running stitch (see page 145), maintaining an even stitch length of approximately ¼ inch. Use your thimble to protect the finger pushing the needle through the quilt fabric.

When you have about 4 inches of thread remaining in the needle, knot the thread as near to the quilt's surface as possible. Insert the needle into the quilt front, and draw it back out again, popping the knot inside. Trim the excess thread. Using a newly threaded needle, continue quilting along the marked lines. When you finish the quilting, knot the thread and pop it inside, as before.

5. Attach Binding
Piece the binding strips, following the directions on page 151. Attach the quilt binding, following the directions for the double-fold binding on page 151.

someone to watch over you

FINISHED MEASUREMENTS
Approximately 32 inches square

MATERIALS
FABRIC 1: ¾ yard of 45-inch-wide light-colored, patterned cotton, for background

FABRIC 2: 2½ yards of 45-inch-wide, darker patterned cotton, for tree trunk, branch, birds, binding, and quilt back

½ yard of lightweight fusible interfacing

Natural, thinnest-loft cotton batting, 46 inches x 36 inches

Cotton thread to blend best with both fabrics (I used light taupe)

Hand-quilting thread to complement both fabrics (I used light gold)

Lap-sized hand-quilting frame

Pattern paper

Fabric scissors

Templates J and K (see pattern sheet page attached to inside back cover of book)

CONSTRUCTION NOTES
Use ¼-inch seam allowances throughout.

This quilt uses a technique for making and turning the raw edges of an appliqué that's similar to the method used to make the Made-By Patch on page 29. I like to think of this as appliqué, although appliqué experts may very well consider it cheating because it uses lightweight fusible interfacing rather than the classic (but challenging) needle-turn method to perfectly fold under the appliqué's edges. Still, the result looks great, and the technique is simple even for novices. Thanks to Heather Ross, a fabric and clothing designer who also teaches at Purl Patchwork, for explaining this technique to me.

1. Prepare Fabric
Wash, dry, and press all fabric.

2. Make Templates
Make **TEMPLATES** J and K from pattern sheet page attached to inside back cover of book. Instead of cutting the templates directly out of this book, trace the pieces on pattern paper, and cut them out of that. Then you'll still have all of the templates in one place, should you ever want to use them again.

3. Cut Fabric
FABRIC 1
Fold the fabric right sides together, and cut one 27-inch-deep piece, selvage to selvage. Trim the selvages, and cut down the width of the piece to make a rectangle measuring 27 inches x 32 inches. Set it aside for the background.

FABRIC 2
Fold the fabric right sides together, and cut one 40-inch-deep piece, selvage to selvage. Trim the selvages to make a 40-inch square, and set it aside for the quilt back.

With the fabric still folded, cut one 14-inch-deep strip, selvage to selvage.

Trim the selvages, and cut down the width of the strip to make a rectangle measuring 14 inches x 32 inches. Set it aside for the tree trunk.

Cut one 16-inch-deep strip, selvage to selvage. Trim the selvages, and cut down the width of the strip to make a rectangle measuring 16 inches x 23 inches. Set it aside for the appliqué.

Cut five 2¼-inch-deep strips, selvage to selvage. Trim the selvages, and set the strips aside for the binding.

3. Make Tree Trunk

This is a great technique for quickly cutting two pieces in one pass that need to fit together along an irregularly shaped edge:

Lay the 27-inch x 32-inch Fabric 1 background piece right side up, with the longer edges running vertically. Place the 14-inch x 32-inch Fabric 2 tree-trunk piece on top, right side up, so that it overlaps the left edge of the Fabric 1 piece by 3 inches. Make sure that the top and bottom edges of the pieces are aligned. Lay **TEMPLATE J** on top of the tree-trunk-fabric piece, aligning the 32-inch straight edge of the template with this fabric's left edge. With your rotary cutter, cut along the curved right edge of the tree-trunk template.

4. Piece Tree Trunk and Background

Carefully pin the cut tree trunk to the cut background, right sides together, using a lot of pins to ease the opposing curved shapes together (before being pinned, the shapes don't look like they'll fit together, but they will; just pin the edges together a little bit at a time). Sew ¼ inch from the pinned edge. Press the seam to the side of the darker fabric.

5. Trace Appliqué

Lay the 16-inch x 23-inch Fabric 2 piece wrong side up. Place **TEMPLATE K** on top, and carefully trace around it with a pencil.

6. Make Appliqué

Lay the interfacing with the fusible side up. Place the Fabric 2 piece you traced in Step 5 over the interfacing, wrong side up, so the traced lines show. Pin the layers together to prevent shifting as you sew. Sew the appliqué fabric and interfacing together all the way around, sewing directly along the traced lines.

Cut a ¼-inch seam allowance around the sewn lines with sharp fabric scissors. To ensure that the seam allowances lie neatly once you've turned the appliqué right side out, clip the seam allowances along the outwardly curving sections of the seam so they don't pull, and cut notches into the seam allowances along the inwardly curving sections of the seam to reduce bulk, cutting very near but not into the seam itself.

Carefully cut into the interfacing along the center of the branch shapes, cutting enough to be able to turn the shape right side out without tearing it. You'll also need to make an additional cut from the center of the branch up into each bird and into the leaves in order to be able to turn all these shapes right side out.

7. Turn Appliqué Right Side Out
Carefully turn the appliqué right side out, using a small, blunt tool such as the base of a small crochet hook to gently push out and shape the points. If necessary, pin through the seam allowance from the appliqué's right side in order to keep it in place and prevent the cut interfacing from slipping down and showing on the front.

Position the appliqué in the desired position on the quilt front, and touch it with a hot iron in a few places to gently fuse the interfacing to the background fabric (anchoring it with the tip of the iron in only a few spots enables you to move the appliqué if you want to reposition it slightly). Once the appliqué is in place, remove any pins you used to hold the seam allowance in place (touching those spots with the tip of your iron to anchor the seam allowance in position), and iron the whole thing to fuse the interfacing securely to the background fabric.

To finish the appliqué, blindstitch (see page 144) by hand around it with the same thread used for piecing the tree trunk to the background. Sew just under the fabric's fold for the most invisible results.

8. Baste Quilt
Baste together the quilt front, batting, and quilt back, following the directions for thread-basting on page 147.

9. Quilt by Hand
I quilted the piece by hand, quilting vertically along the trunk and horizontally in the sky. In addition, I quilted around the outside of the appliqué to make it pop forward. I began by quilting along the seam of the trunk and then around the appliqué. Then I quilted in roughly parallel lines about 3 inches apart, working vertically along the trunk and horizontally across the background fabric. I continued quilting between these parallel lines until they were about ¾ inches to 1 inch apart. For detailed information on hand-quilting, see page 149.

10. Piece and Attach Binding
Piece binding strips, following the directions on page 151. Attach the binding, following the directions for the double-fold binding on page 151.

(sort of) crazy quilt

FINISHED MEASUREMENTS
Approximately 30 inches x
35 inches

MATERIALS
FABRIC 1: ¼ yard each of an
assortment of 45-inch-wide, hand-
dyed and/or commercially dyed
cottons (about 2 yards total) in a
close range of colors, for piecing

FABRIC 2: 1¼ yards of 45-inch-
wide solid cotton, for inner border
and quilt back

FABRIC 3: ½ yard each of three
45-inch-wide, hand-dyed and/or
commercially dyed cottons in
different but closely related colors,
for outer border

FABRIC 4: ½ yard of 45-inch-wide
solid cotton, for binding

Cotton thread for machine-piecing
to blend best with all fabrics

Hand-quilting thread to
complement most fabrics
(I used a salmon color)

Hand-quilting needles
(I prefer size 10 betweens)

Thimble

Natural, thinnest-loft cotton batting,
46 inches x 36 inches

Big, brown paper bag

CONSTRUCTION NOTES
Use ¼-inch seam allowances
throughout.

The steps for making this quilt are a meeting of the order I
love and the freedom that inspires me in the work of other
quiltmakers, in particular, the quilters of Gee's Bend and
Denyse Schmidt. I am very thankful to Denyse for intro-
ducing me to her paper-bag technique, which I used to
construct the center panel. This project was hand-quilted
by Cassandra Thoreson, a very talented craftsperson,
teacher, and friend. I was thrilled to have her quilt it, and
I love the lively character of the work she did.

1. Prepare Fabric
Wash, dry, and press all fabric. If you're using hand-dyed fabric, it's very
important that you follow this step to prevent the dyes from running.
(Remember, even wall-hanging quilts need to be washed once in a while!)

2. Cut Fabric
FABRIC 1
Fold one Fabric 1 piece selvage to selvage. Trim the selvages, and trim the
fold to make two rectangles measuring approximately 9 inches x 20 inches.
Cut each rectangle into strips along the 20-inch length, in a range of widths
from about ¾ inch to 3 inches. Cut the strips freehand (without your ruler), but
try to cut in relatively straight lines (not too curved). Repeat the process with
the remaining Fabric 1 pieces. This will give you more than enough strips for
piecing the center panel.

FABRIC 2
Cut two 1-inch-deep strips, selvage to selvage. Trim the selvages, and set
the strips aside for the inner border. Cut one 38-inch-deep piece, selvage to
selvage. Trim the selvages, and set the piece aside for the quilt back. Use
the excess fabric for the center panel, if desired.

FABRIC 3
This quilt has a 6-inch-deep outer border around its top and sides, and a
12-inch-deep outer border at the bottom (made of two 6-inch-wide strips).
The border varies in color around the quilt since it is pieced from several
close colors.

To create the border pieces, fold one Fabric 3 piece selvage to selvage, and cut two 6½-inch-deep strips. Trim the selvages, and trim the fold to make six rectangles about 6½ inches x 20 inches. Set the rectangles aside. Repeat the process with the remaining Fabric 3 pieces. I also suggest cutting a few of these strips in half widthwise to mix up the border even more for piecing in Step 6. Use the excess fabric for the center panel, if desired.

FABRIC 4
Cut five 2¼-inch-deep strips, selvage to selvage. Trim the selvages, and set the strips aside for the binding. Use the excess fabric for the center panel, if desired.

3. Make Center Panel Pieces
Mix the Fabric 1 strips together and place them in a paper bag. Pull two or three strips from the bag (no looking!), and sew them together along their 20-inch side. Repeat the process until you've used all the strips.

Return the sewn Fabric 1 pairs to the bag. Then pull out two pairs, and sew them together along their 20-inch side. Repeat until you have a lot of different-looking pieces, each with four to six strips sewn together.

Next, cut each piece freehand into smaller pieces in a range of widths from about 1 inch to 8 inches, cutting perpendicular to the seams. This will give you more than enough pieces for your center panel.

4. Sew Center Panel
If there are any pieces you really don't like, remove them. Sort the remaining pieces into three piles according to their widths: small, medium, and large. Set aside your favorite small piece (Piece 1) and return the remaining small pieces to the bag. Select one piece (Piece 2) out of the bag and sew it to Piece 1, joining any side you like. If Piece 2 is shorter than the side you are sewing it to on Piece 1, pick another piece out of the bag and sew it to the end of Piece 2, and then sew the resulting piece to Piece 1. Once you've sewn the pieces together, trim the excess fabric freehand; but cut in a relatively straight line. Press the seam to the side of each newly added piece.

Lay the patch you've made right side up, with the seam you just sewed on the left. Pick another small piece out of the bag, and sew it, right sides together, to the top of your patch, adding length again to the new piece you're attaching if necessary. Trim the excess, and press the seam to the side of the newly added piece, as above.

Keep repeating this process, adding the pile of medium-sized pieces to the bag when you're about halfway through the small pieces and adding the large pieces to the bag when you're about halfway through the medium pieces, until you've made a rectangular center panel no smaller than 16½ inches x 17½ inches. When your panel is large enough, square it up (see page 139) to measure 16½ inches x 17½ inches.

5. Add Inner Border

Lay the center panel right side up. Pin one 1-inch Fabric 2 strip to one edge of the panel, right sides together, and sew ¼ inch from the pinned edge. Trim the excess, and press the seam away from the center panel. Lay the piece right side up, with the seam you just sewed to the left. Pin the second Fabric 2 strip to the top of the piece, and sew the two together, as above. Repeat to join the remaining two Fabric 2 strips to the panel.

6. Piece Outer Border Strips

Use the paper-bag technique from piecing the center panel to help you mix up your Fabric 3 colors. Piece the strips along their 6½-inch sides as necessary, to make four 24½-inch-wide strips and one 30½-inch-wide strip.

7. Add Outer Border

Lay the center panel right side up. Align and pin one 24½-inch-wide Fabric 3 strip to the top of the piece, right sides together, and sew the two ¼ inch from the pinned edge. Trim the excess and press the seam away from the center panel.

Lay the center panel right side up, with the seam you just sewed to the left. Pin a second 24½-inch-wide Fabric 3 strip to the top of the piece, and sew ¼ inch from the pinned edge. Trim the excess and press the seam away from the center panel. Repeat this step twice more to join the two remaining 24½-inch-wide Fabric 3 strips to the last two sides of the center panel. Then join the 30½-inch-wide strip along the bottom of the panel, so the bottom border is twice as wide as the other borders.

8. Baste Quilt

Baste together the quilt front, batting, and quilt back, following the directions for thread-basting on page 147.

9. Quilt by Hand

Follow the directions for hand-quilting and the rocking method of stitching on page 150. This quilt was quilted freehand following the larger shapes of the piecing. You could also stitch-in-the-ditch (see page 148) and then in concentric rectangles, or take an allover approach and quilt it in a grid. Whatever you do, try to make it fun! I recommend quilting continuously across the quilt rather than focusing on one area at a time, so that you can decide to be done at any point.

10. Attach Binding

Piece the binding strips, following the directions on page 151. Then attach the binding, following the directions for the double-fold binding on page 151.

log cabin quilt

This quilt is a variation on traditional log-cabin quilts. It has a center rectangle, rather than a square, and the blocks are arranged in an off-center diamond pattern featuring a floral print from Amy Butler with beautiful, sweeping lines. I've always loved log cabin quilts and can hardly imagine creating a quilt book without at least one log cabin design in it. But the log cabin design doesn't naturally lend itself to "last-minute" projects, since it typically involves a lot of labor. For this project, I've included very specific instructions for folding and cutting the fabric, so you can make the pieces for this quilt in the most efficient way possible. The pieced blocks are chain-pieced together, another time-saving technique.

FINISHED MEASUREMENTS
Approximately 80 inches x 96 inches

MATERIALS
FABRIC 1: 5 yards of 45-inch-wide floral cotton, for piecing

FABRIC 2: 3½ yards of 45-inch-wide solid cotton, for piecing

FABRIC 3: 2½ yards of 108-inch-wide quilter's muslin (or approximately 7 yards of 45-inch-wide cotton), for quilt back

Two large spools of cotton thread to match Fabric 2

Natural, thinnest-loft cotton batting, 108 inches x 93 inches

CONSTRUCTION NOTES
Use ¼-inch seam allowances throughout.

1. Prepare Fabric
Wash, dry, and press all fabric.

2. Cut Quilt Back
Fold the quilter's muslin selvage to selvage, and cut one 88-inch-deep piece. Trim the selvages, so the piece measures 88 inches deep x 104 inches wide. Set the cut fabric aside for the quilt back.

3. Cut Doubled Strips for Front
Fold your fabric from selvage to selvage, and then fold its length in half, so that you can cut two strips at a time. (Do not be tempted to fold the fabric's length in half first and then fold the fabric selvage to selvage. You'll end up with short cuts if you do it this way—believe me, I tried!) Be sure that the folded edges of the two layers stay exactly aligned, even if your selvages get slightly misaligned. Once you cut the doubled strips, set them aside very carefully. Because you'll be making further cuts from the strips, you'll want to keep their folded ends and cut edges as precisely aligned as possible.

FABRIC 1
Cut five 2¼-inch-deep doubled strips, selvage to selvage, which yields a total of ten 2¼-inch-deep strips. Trim the selvages, and set the doubled strips aside for the binding.

Cut three 4½-inch-deep doubled strips, selvage to selvage, which yields a total of six 4½-inch-deep strips total. Carefully set the doubled strips aside for making further cuts.

Cut twenty-six 2½-inch-deep doubled strips, selvage to selvage, for a total of fifty-two 2½-inch-deep strips. Carefully set the doubled strips aside for making further cuts.

Cut twenty-five 2½-inch-deep doubled strips, selvage to selvage, which yields a total of fifty 2½-inch-deep strips total. Carefully set the doubled strips aside for making further cuts.

4. Make Second Cuts for Piecing

FABRIC 1

Center Rectangles

Working with the three doubled 4½-inch-deep Fabric 1 strips (six strips total), start with the first doubled strip: Trim its selvages, and make three 6½-inch-wide cuts, for a total of twelve 4½-inch-deep x 6½-inch-wide pieces. Repeat with remaining two doubled strips for a total of thirty-six pieces. Discard six of these, and set the remaining thirty Center Rectangles aside for piecing.

Log Cabin Strips

Working with eight of the doubled 2½-inch-deep Fabric 1 strips (sixteen strips total), start with the first doubled strip: Trim its selvages and then make two 8½-inch-wide cuts, producing a total of eight 2½-inch-deep x 8½-inch-wide pieces. Repeat with the remaining seven doubled strips for a total of sixty-four pieces. Discard four of these, and set the remaining sixty Log Cabin Strips aside for piecing.

Working with ten of the doubled 2½-inch-deep Fabric 1 strips (twenty strips total), begin the cuts from the folded edge and do not trim the fold, to ensure that you get enough mileage from your strips! With the first doubled strip, make one cut 6¼ inches from the fold, and another cut 12½ inches from the first cut, producing six 2½-inch-deep x 12½-inch-wide pieces. Repeat with the remaining nine doubled strips for a total of sixty pieces. Set these Log Cabin Strips aside for piecing.

Working with the eight remaining doubled 2½-inch-deep Fabric 1 strips (sixteen strips total), start with the first doubled strip: Trim the selvages, and then make one 16½-inch-wide cut, producing four 2½-inch-deep x 16½-inch-wide pieces. Repeat with the remaining seven doubled strips for a total of thirty-two pieces. Discard two of these, and set the remaining thirty Log Cabin Strips aside for piecing.

FABRIC 2

Log Cabin Strips

Working with five of the doubled 2½-inch-deep Fabric 2 strips (ten strips total), start with the first doubled strip: Trim the selvage and then make three 6½-inch-wide cuts, producing twelve 2½-inch-deep x 6½-inch-wide pieces. Repeat with the remaining four doubled strips for a total of sixty pieces. Set these Log Cabin Strips aside for piecing.

Working with another five of the doubled Fabric 2 strips (ten strips total), begin the cuts from folded edge and do not trim the fold to insure that you get enough mileage from your strips. With the first doubled strip, make one cut 5¼ inches from the fold, and another cut 10½ inches from the first cut, for a total of six 2½-inch-deep x 10½-inch-wide pieces. Repeat these cuts with the remaining four doubled strips, producing a total of thirty pieces. Set these Log Cabin Strips aside for piecing.

Working with remaining fifteen doubled Fabric 2 strips (thirty strips total), again begin the cuts from the folded edge and do not trim the fold. With the first doubled strip, make one cut 5¼ inches from fold, and another cut 14½ inches from the first cut, producing two 2½-inch-deep x 10½-inch-wide pieces and four 2½-inch-deep x 14½-inch-wide pieces. Repeat these cuts with the remaining fourteen doubled strips for a total of thirty 2½-inch-deep x 10 ½-inch-wide pieces and sixty 2½-inch-deep x 14½-inch-wide pieces. Set these Log Cabin Strips aside for piecing.

5. Prepare for Piecing

This quilt is made of thirty blocks that are exactly the same (see Diagram A). The final design depends on how you situate each block within the grid, a process known as "setting" your blocks. But beware! Because of the way the cuts were made, half of your Fabric 1 pieces will be face up and half of them will be face down. If you think you can keep track of this while you are piecing your top, more power to you. For me, it made a lot of sense to take a minute to turn them all face up before piecing.

To prepare for piecing, organize your strips from smallest to largest.

Diagram A

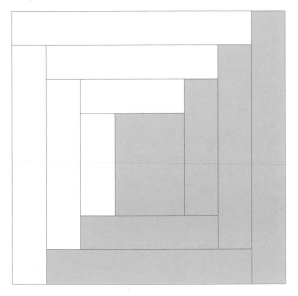

Each block of this quilt is assembled in exactly the same way (as shown here). However, there are numerous ways to assemble the blocks and create different effects (See Diagrams B and C on page 125).

You will always add strips to the piece in a counter-clockwise manner, and always prepare to add the next strip by positioning the most recently sewn seam running along the left side. If you happen to get the piecing turned around, or put it aside and pick it up later, you can always identify the most recently sewn seam because it runs along one full side of the piece and has no other seams crossing it.

6. Piece Blocks

STEP 1 Sew one 6½-inch-wide Fabric 2 Log Cabin Strip to the 6½-inch edge of each Fabric 1 Center Rectangle, right sides together. Using the chain-piecing technique (see page 143), sew through all thirty blocks. Clip the threads between blocks to separate them. Press the seams toward the center rectangle.

STEP 2 Turn the blocks so that the seam you just sewed is on the left. Pin one 6½-inch-wide Fabric 2 Log Cabin Strip to the top of each block. Chain-piece all thirty blocks. Clip the threads between blocks to separate them. Press the seams away from the center rectangle.

STEP 3 Turn the blocks so that the seam you just sewed is on the left. Pin one 8½-inch-wide Fabric 1 Log Cabin Strip to the top of each block. Chain-piece all thirty blocks. Clip the threads between blocks to separate them. Press the seams away from the center rectangle.

STEP 4 Repeat Step 3.

STEP 5 Turn the block so that the seam you just sewed is on the left. Pin one 10½-inch-wide Fabric 2 Log Cabin Strip to the top of each block. Chain-piece all thirty blocks. Clip the threads between blocks to separate them. Press the seams away from the center rectangle.

STEP 6 Repeat Step 5.

STEP 7 Turn the block so that the seam you just sewed is on the left. Pin one 12½-inch-wide Fabric 1 Log Cabin Strip to the top of each block. Chain-piece all thirty blocks. Clip the threads between blocks to separate them. Press the seams away from the center rectangle.

STEP 8 Repeat Step 7.

STEP 9 Turn the blocks so that the seam you just sewed is on the left. Pin one 14½-inch-wide Fabric 2 Log Cabin Strip to the top of each block. Chain-piece all thirty blocks. Clip the threads between blocks to separate them. Press the seams away from the center rectangle.

STEP 10 Repeat Step 9.

STEP 11 Turn the blocks so that the seam you just sewed is on the left. Pin one 16½-inch-wide Fabric 1 Log Cabin Strip to the top of each block. Chain-piece all thirty blocks. Clip the threads between blocks to separate them. Press the seams away from the center rectangle.

Diagram B

I call this layout an "off-center diamond."
This is how my quilt is set.

Diagram C

This layout is traditionally known as the
"straight furrow variation," and is another
option for setting your quilt.

7. Lay Out Quilt Front

There are many ways to lay out this quilt front. I laid mine out to form an off-center diamond (see Diagram B). You could also lay your blocks out to make a "straight furrow variation" (see Diagram C). Since each block is the same, it's all about how you put them together. Whatever design you choose, just make sure that you mark your blocks before you begin sewing them together! For a quilt like this, I usually lay everything out and then pin a little tag on each block with a safety pin to identify its position in the layout.

This quilt is laid out in five columns and six rows: The first column is A, the second is B, the third is C, the fourth is D, and the fifth is E. Each row is numbered, 1 to 6, so the block in the upper left corner is designated A-1, and the block in the lower right corner E-6. If you pin little tags with these labels at the top of your blocks before sewing, it will help keep your blocks organized as you assemble your quilt front.

8. Assemble Quilt Front

Sew the bottom of the first block (A-1) to the top of the second (A-2), right sides together. Continue sewing blocks by chain-piecing them together as follows: B-1 to B-2, C-1 to C-2, D-1 to D-2, and E-1 to E-2. Next, chain-piece A-3 to A-4, B-3 to B-4, C-3 to C-4, D-3 to D-4, and E-3 to E-4. Then, chain-piece A-5 to A-6, B-5 to B-6, C-5 to C-6, D-5 to D-6, and E-5 to E-6.

When you're sewing your blocks together, you'll find that a few intersecting seams are pressed in the same direction. As you come to these seams, reverse the direction that the seam is pressed on one of the blocks in order to avoid having a big lump to quilt through when you're finished (I reposition these seam allowances by finger-pressing them—see page 144).

Once you've sewn all the pairs together, lay out your blocks again just to check their position. Then continue chain-piecing the rows together, and then the columns together, until you've completed piecing the quilt front.

9. Baste Quilt

Baste together the quilt front, batting, and quilt back, following the directions for pin-basting on page 147.

10. Machine-Quilt

I quilted my log cabin diamond quilt by stitching-in-the-ditch (see page 148). There are a lot of seams to sew through on this quilt, so I recommend starting by stitching-in-the-ditch between the blocks, and then around each center rectangle. If you want to continue quilting in each ditch after that, you can; but even if you don't, your piece will be quilted enough to hold the batting in place.

11. Piece and Attach Binding

Piece the 2¼-inch-deep Fabric 1 binding strips, following the directions on page 151. Then attach the binding, following the directions for the double-fold binding on page 151.

patchwork + quilting basics

MATERIALS

I always recommend using the best-quality materials that you can afford for quilting. Spending precious time making something with less-than-wonderful materials can produce disappointing results. I find natural materials to be the most inspiring, vibrant, and timeless, so I use them almost exclusively.

Fabric

If you look through almost any book about patchwork and quilting, including this one, you might notice that they advise readers to use plain-weave cotton in their projects almost exclusively. This is because plain-weave cotton is typically the easiest type of fabric to work with—it doesn't slip or stretch as you sew it, as some other fabrics do—and it comes in thousands of different colors and prints. Traditional quilts are made from a variety of materials, most often cotton but also wools and silks. You can use almost any type of fabric for the projects in this book, but if you decide to substitute a wool fabric in place of cotton, or a twill weave instead of a plain-weave, be aware that your results will be different from mine. Of course, when you're making your own projects, this is part of the adventure! But if you're new to patchwork and quilting, I recommend using plain-weave cottons to start with; and then, after you've mastered the basic techniques, you can explore working with other fabrics. If you have more experience and an adventurous spirit, anything goes. You can mix together any type of fiber and weave in your quilts.

COTTON

Cotton, especially plain-weave cotton, tends to be the easiest type of fabric to sew with because it does not stretch or slip as you sew it. It is also easy to care for. Most quilt shops carry primarily plain-weave cottons, and many of the larger chain fabric stores have designated quilting sections featuring plain-weave cottons as well.

Plain-weave cottons meant for quilting are usually 45 inches wide; and, for most of the projects in this book, I recommend buying 45-inch-wide yardage (each pattern includes yardage requirements). Sometimes, however, only a small piece of fabric is required, and in some cases a ¼-yard cut (9 inches deep x by 45 inches wide) is what's called for. But a narrow, ¼-yard piece isn't always appropriate, especially if the main part of the print's design is deeper than 9 inches. This is where *fat quarters* come in. The brainchild of a very clever quilter, a fat quarter measures approximately 18 inches deep by 22½ inches wide, meaning that it provides the same amount of square inches as a regular ¼ yard of fabric but is cut twice as deep and half as wide.

A few of the patterns call for quilter's muslin. Although most muslin, a kind of cotton, is used only for developing and making patterns, quilter's muslin is of a very high quality and can be used in finished projects. Quilter's muslin comes in three widths—45 inches, 56 inches, and 108 inches—and most quilt shops carry all of them.

Another kind of cotton called for in a few patterns is printable cotton, that is, plain cotton fabric whose surface has been specially treated to accept the inks from an inkjet printer. The printed fabric is fully washable, and the inks are permanent. The printable cotton I prefer comes from The Electric Quilt Company (see Sources for Supplies on page 156) in packs of six or more sheets sized to fit in an inkjet printer. This is a great product to use when you want to personalize a patchwork or quilted gift with a message, as I did on the Happy Birthday Pillow on page 58.

SILK

Silk is a gorgeous, vibrant fabric but can be very slippery and difficult to sew. However, I've found that if you machine-wash and -dry silk before using it, the finished piece is not only easier to care for but the silk is easier to handle. For quilts, I recommend using heavyweight silk like silk taffeta because it wears beautifully and isn't as delicate as some other fine silks. If you plan to piece silks with cotton, be sure to wash and dry both fabrics ahead of time so that you can launder your finished piece easily.

WOOL

I haven't used wool fabric in this book, but lots of vintage quilts, particularly Amish quilts, are made with wool. Wool fabric is delightful to sew with. It has a gorgeous hand (meaning that it feels great when touched) and wears well. However, wool that has not been treated for washing can felt when washed, so test a sample before you begin. Or, if you like, you can make entire projects out of an assortment of beautiful felted wools.

VINTAGE

One way to make a project extra special and personal is to incorporate rare vintage fabrics from a flea market or antique shop (or maybe from an older relative's long-saved fabric stash). I like this idea in theory but offer a few words of caution: Vintage fabrics tend to shrink and bleed more than newer fabrics. If you want to use vintage fabrics in your projects, wash and dry them before use to preshrink them and set their dyes. Then do a bleed test (see page 138) before incorporating these fabrics into your beloved creation.

Thread

I recommend using the highest-quality thread available at all times. The conventional wisdom is to use thread with the same fiber content as your fabric or a fiber that's slightly weaker than your fabric so that, over time, your thread won't damage or tear the fabric. There are exceptions, of course; for instance, pure silk thread, which reflects light beautifully and is very strong, is a nice treat for topstitching on almost any type of fabric. For sewing by hand and machine, however, my favorite thread is Gütermann's 100-percent cotton thread. This thread is very fine and comes in an amazing range of colors.

When I buy thread, I usually buy three spools of the color I'm using. I use one spool to thread the machine, the second to make bobbins with, and the third to keep in reserve for both of the first two needs. This way, I have my bobbins all set to go, so when one runs out, I can replace it quickly without having to stop, unthread my machine to thread a new bobbin, and then rethread my machine.

For hand-quilting, I always use thread specifically designed for this purpose. Hand-quilting thread is thicker than standard sewing thread and is glazed with a waxy coating that keeps it from getting tangled and grips the fabric, making the stitches readily visible. However, because this waxy coating can build up inside your machine's moving parts and damage the machine, do *not* use hand-quilting thread for machine-sewing or -quilting. Instead use regular cotton sewing thread.

And for either hand- or machine-quilting, don't be tempted to use vintage thread. Although the colors of vintage threads and their beautiful, old wooden spools can be seductive, thread that's been around for a long time tends to become brittle and break easily, which can create problems in your sewing machine by putting uneven tension on its moving parts.

Within the quilting community, there's a lot of debate about whether to use polyester thread with cotton fabrics. Some quilters think that polyester thread is too strong for the cotton fibers in the fabric and will eventually "saw" though and damage them; others refute this claim and sew only with polyester thread because they consider it a universal fiber that works with any kind of fabric. For me, it's a matter of personal aesthetics. I love the feel and quality of natural fibers and choose not to use synthetic fibers anywhere in my work.

Batting

Batting is the insulating layer that goes between the quilt's top and backing. Batting is most often made of wool or cotton but can be made of any material. For lightweight summer quilts, for example, you might use a layer of cotton flannel for batting; some vintage quilts have older, worn-out quilts inside of them serving as batting.

When purchasing batting, there are a couple of factors to consider: First is the size of your quilt. Always buy batting that's at least 4 inches larger in all directions than your quilt top so that you'll have enough batting to complete your quilt. Avoid sewing smaller bits of batting together to create a large enough piece for your quilt top since this will cause lumps in your quilt. Most quilt shops sell batting in sizes that correspond to mattress sizes; and some of them, especially larger shops, sell batting by the yard on rolls.

The second factor to consider is the loft, or density, of your batting. Wool batting generally comes in only one loft, but cotton batting comes in many different lofts. I prefer to use the thinnest-loft cotton batting I can find because it's easy to quilt, both by hand and machine, and isn't too heavy, which is an especially important consideration for large projects. Most traditional quilts are quilted with a very thin-loft,100-percent cotton batting. If you're a beginning quilter, you may be surprised by the thinness of some cotton battings; and when you think of quilts, what may come to mind are big, fluffy comforters and down jackets. If you want that kind of loft, I recommend wool batting rather than a thicker-loft cotton batting, which will only give you a heavier quilt that still isn't fluffy. My favorite batting comes from Quilter's

Dream, and I'm especially fond of their very thin Request Loft cotton batting and their Dream Wool batting (see Sources for Supplies on page 156).

In contrast to thin-loft cotton batting, heavyweight (or high-loft) cotton batting is great for projects that need some body, and it can replace heavy interfacing in bags or other craft projects. The Quilted Coasters on page 20 use this high-loft cotton batting.

Also keep in mind that high-quality batting doesn't contain any fillers like scrim (a very fine, often synthetic, layer on the top of the batting), binders, or glue, which are often added to lesser-quality cotton battings to hold the fibers together. As well, high-quality batting doesn't require prewashing, nor does the finished project shrink when washed.

I don't recommend using polyester batting. Although it's lofty and lightweight, it "beards," meaning that the fiber works its way out of the quilt through the seams and tiny needle punctures in your fabric caused by sewing, creating an unsightly fuzz that's next to impossible to remove. If you want a lightweight or lofty batting, use wool.

Stuffing

I love the feel of natural cotton stuffing in toys, pincushions, or other stuffed projects, and my favorite stuffing is made by Quilter's Dream and sold at most quilt shops. The density and weight of cotton stuffing lends toys an old-fashioned quality and keeps pincushions stable. If you're accustomed to using polyfill for stuffing, you may be surprised by the lumpiness of cotton stuffing. The secret is to pull the cotton apart a bit before using it. Also when stuffing a project with cotton stuffing, I generally use a knitting needle or crochet hook to really push the stuffing into all of the nooks and crannies.

TOOLS

Below is a list of the tools that I use regularly and consider essential for the projects in this book. Keep in mind that, for just about any need, a clever quilter has invented a tool, template, or special ruler, so there are many additional tools available.

Measuring and Marking Tools

CLEAR RULERS

Clear plastic rulers ensure precise measurements and very straight cuts, and are used with rotary cutters and cutting mats. These rulers come in a range of sizes, and every brand seems to have its own style for indicating measurements. For rotary cutting, a 6½-inch x 24½-inch ruler (or its near equivalent, since sizes vary slightly from brand to brand) is large enough to cut standard 45-inch-wide quilting fabric from selvage to selvage; this is the ruler that you'll use most often.

I also use a 12½-inch square ruler for squaring up fabric (see page 139) and a small 4½-inch x 8½-inch ruler for cutting lots of tiny pieces. When selecting a ruler, be sure that you understand how its measurements are indicated and that you can see the edge of your fabric clearly through its markings. I prefer Creative Grids rulers because their markings are very thin and easy to see through. They also have a non-slip feature on the back to keep the ruler from moving when you're cutting.

CIRCULAR TEMPLATES

To mark accurate and precise curves on fabric, it's useful to have a set of circular templates. You can always use a circular object, such as a soup can or dessert plate instead, but the nice thing about circular templates is that they indicate exactly where the center of your circle will be. A non-slip feature on the back of the templates also prevents slipping as you trace around them.

I recommend the circular templates from Creative Grids because they come in a set of five sizes ranging from 2½ inches to 6½ inches in diameter, with each template exactly 1 inch larger than the next. When cutting circles and curves, I prefer to use scissors rather than a rotary cutter (see page 141 for more on cutting curves).

TEMPLATE PLASTIC

Template plastic is a thin, translucent flexible plastic used for making reusable templates. It's available in most fabric and quilt shops in single sheets or packs of three to five sheets, ranging in size from 8½ inches x 11½ inches to 18 inches x 24 inches. There are many weights of template plastic available, and the thicker the plastic, the more rigid it is. If your design is very simple in shape, the thicker plastic is nice because it's very easy to trace

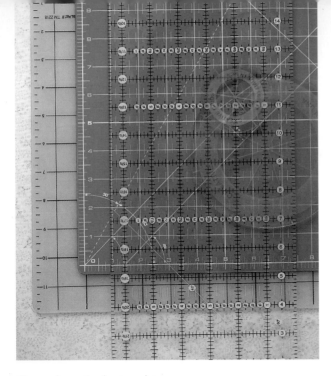

Clear rulers, circular templates,
and self-healing cutting mats.

around. For more complex shapes, the thinner version is easier to cut. To use template plastic, trace over your design with a fine permanent marker, then cut it out with the scissors you use for cutting paper.

PATTERN PAPER

There are several kinds of pattern paper available, and the one I like to work with is a very thin, inexpensive paper that feels like tissue paper but is much stronger. It's used to trace shapes that are too large or complex for template plastic (see above), such as the outer arc of the Color-Wheel Quilt (see page 107).

Available in traditional dressmaking-fabric shops and some quilt stores, pattern paper is usually sold in 30-inch-wide, 10-yard-long rolls and sometimes in precut sheets. The manufacturer's label should say that the paper can be marked with a pencil and erased easily without tearing.

FABRIC MARKERS

It's sometimes necessary to mark your fabric so that you know exactly where to cut or sew. The best way to decide between the many available types of fabric markers is to try out a few. I like Clover's *hera* marker, a dense plastic tool that leaves a visible crease on the fabric rather than the colored line made by some markers. I always use a *hera* marker to mark my quilting lines before I start quilting. If I find that the *hera* marker doesn't leave a clear enough crease on a single layer of fabric, I use a pencil with a fine point and soft lead to mark the lines on the fabric's wrong side.

I don't like to use ink markers on my quilts, although plenty of quilters find them useful. Some of the inks in these markers are washable and others disappear; if you choose to use an ink marker, be sure to test its washability on your fabric before marking up your project.

Cutting Tools

ROTARY CUTTER

This tool resembles a pizza cutter but has a rotary blade designed for fabric. It cuts straight edges more quickly and precisely than scissors, and can be used on several layers of fabric at once. An important quilting tool, the rotary cutter is best used with a few basic precautions in order to avoid injuries. For a full list of these important safety guidelines, see page 139.

I prefer the Deluxe Olfa 45mm rotary cutter, but there's a range of brands and sizes available. I get the most use out of a 45mm blade, but smaller blades can be handy for cutting tiny shapes, as can larger blades for longer cuts. The main things to consider when selecting a rotary cutter are whether it features a basic safety mechanism and whether replacement blades are available. If you're left-handed, be sure to check to see that the cutter can be set for left-handed use.

Some Quilter's Tools
1. Emery cushion
2. Thimbles
3. Seam ripper
4. *Hera* marker
5. Scissors
6. Rotary cutter
7. Embroidery scissors
8. Binding clips
9. Bent-arm safety pins

SELF-HEALING CUTTING MAT

A self-healing cutting mat should always be used with a rotary cutter for several reasons: It protects your work surface from the rotary cutter's sharp blade; its soft, yet resilient surface protects the blade from damage; and the mat "self-heals" after every cut, so its surface stays smooth and your cuts remain accurate over time.

Most mats have a printed grid on only one side but can be used on either side. If you find the grid confusing, turn the mat over so that the plain side faces up.

Cutting mats are available in a range of sizes. I recommend one that's at least 18 inches x 24 inches, because the 24-inch length is necessary for cutting your fabric from selvage to selvage. If you have the room, a 24-inch x 36-inch mat is even better. I like the cutting mats made by Omnigrid; their slightly matte surface prevents fabric from slipping and continues to self-heal after years of use.

SCISSORS

I recommend keeping three pairs of scissors in your work area: one reserved for cutting fabric, one for cutting thread, and one for cutting paper and template plastic. I use 8-inch dressmaking shears for fabric, 4-inch embroidery scissors for thread, and 8-inch scissors for paper and template plastic.

My choice for fabric scissors is Gingher brand, whose tools are exquisitely made and worth their cost. Fiskars also makes good-quality fabric scissors at very affordable prices, and I also like their paper scissors for cutting paper and template plastic. If you're left-handed, get scissors made for left-handed use.

And since all scissors tend to grow dull after prolonged use, check with local fabric shops for sharpening services.

Pins and Pinning Tools

I confess that I love my pins—they make my seams nice and clean, allow me to align intersecting points precisely, and help keep my work organized.

STRAIGHT PINS

There are many types of straight pins—long and short; thick and thin;—and with metal, plastic, glass, and even "flowered" heads. You can find all of these types of pins in most quilt shops.

For patchwork, very thin pins with glass heads are best since they'll keep your fabric from shifting as you work and won't leave marks on your fabric. Their glass heads are easy to pull out as you sew and won't melt under the heat of the iron. Clover makes wonderful, very fine patchwork pins with glass heads in two different colors, which can be handy if you need to keep track of a point, such as the beginning or ending of a seam. However, if you're working with heavyweight fabric, like canvas, denim, or upholstery-weight fabric, use a pin that's thicker than a glass-head pin. You'll find these thicker pins at almost any fabric shop and sometimes even in the sewing section of your local drugstore.

PINCUSHION

It's helpful to keep your pins in a handy spot near your sewing machine, and a pincushion serves this need perfectly. A good pincushion should be heavy enough to stay still when you stick your pins in it. I prefer a wide pincushion that I can keep in the same spot next to my sewing machine, so that I can pull out pins and place them in the cushion as I sew without having to look at it.

EMERY CUSHION

Pins can be expensive and, after repeated use, can become dull. An emery cushion is a piece of fabric filled with grains of emery that help sharpen your pins (like the strawberry-shaped emery cushion in your grandmother's sewing kit). To sharpen a pin, just stick it into an emery cushion several times, and then test it on a scrap of fabric. Repeat the process, if necessary.

Needles and Thimbles

While sewing by hand is very simple, you'll get the best results with each technique by using a needle specifically designed for that purpose. Below are descriptions of the needles I use regularly:

SHARPS

Sharps are the closest thing to an all-purpose needle there is. They're useful for closing seams, appliqué work, hand-piecing, and a variety of other simple techniques.

SASHIKO NEEDLES

Sashiko needles are traditionally used in Japan for hand-quilting. These needles are much longer than Western quilting needles, so they take larger stitches and can produce a more rustic look. Since the eye of a sashiko needle is big enough to accommodate thicker threads, this needle is a great choice for quilting with embroidery thread.

QUILTING BETWEENS

Quilting betweens are very short needles that take tiny stitches. This needle's short length lends itself to the "rocking technique" (see page 149) used in hand-quilting.

CURVED QUILTING NEEDLES

Curved quilting needles are wonderful for thread-basting (see page 147). When you thread-baste a quilt, it can be challenging to pull a regular, straight needle back up through the quilt since the layers of fabric are pulled taut. By contrast, a curved needle can be easily pulled to the working surface.

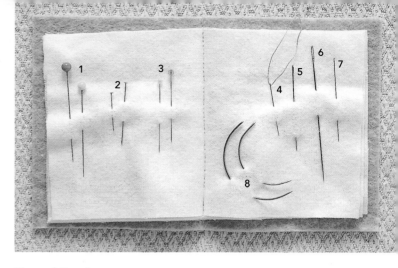

Pins and Needles
1. Large glass head pins for heavy fabrics
2. Applique pins
3. Fine glass head patchwork pins
4. Size 10 between hand-quilting needle
5. Sharp hand-sewing needle
6. Sashiko needle
7. Milliner's needle
8. Curved quilting needles

THIMBLES

A thimble is a small tool that fits over your finger to protect it when pushing the needle through the fabric. Thimbles are available in various materials, including leather, metal, and plastic. I use a leather thimble because it allows me to feel what I'm doing better than other types.

Many quilters also use a second thimble to protect the finger on the other hand held under the quilt to receive the needle's point. I prefer to use a small, metal, stick-on "under thimble" for this purpose.

Sewing Machine and Accessories

SEWING MACHINE

There are many reasonably priced machines on the market that work very well and have all the features necessary for completing the projects in this book. In addition to sewing plain straight seams, you should be able to back-stitch and make a zigzag stitch with your machine, and you should be able to set the stitch to different lengths.

Also, you'll need a walking foot (see below) and a ¼-inch presser foot. Not all machines come with these two important accessories, but they can usually be purchased separately. For help buying a sewing machine or accessories, I suggest calling your local quilt shop. If the shop doesn't carry machines or accessories, they'll likely be able to recommend a local resource that does.

WALKING FOOT

A walking foot is the attachment used for machine-quilting. It guides all three layers of a quilt through the machine evenly, preventing tucks and pulls in the finished work. If your machine doesn't have a walking foot, check to see if the manufacturer offers one. Otherwise, buy a universal walking foot. Your walking foot will most likely come with a seam guide-bar attachment tool. This is a great tool for measuring parallel quilting lines without having to mark your quilt ahead of time.

UNIVERSAL SEWING-MACHINE NEEDLES

There are numerous kinds of sewing-machine needles for various tasks. A universal sewing-machine needle, as the name implies, works on almost any type of fabric. Regardless of brand, the packaging will indicate that the needle is a universal one. I keep several extra universal needles on hand at all times in case my needle breaks or starts to feel dull mid-project. Occasionally, even a brand new needle can cause problems. If your thread keeps breaking or your stitches look uneven, one of the first things to do is to replace your needle. In fact, I change my needle before every new project. Although universal needles work for most fabrics, a denim needle is more appropriate when sewing a heavyweight fabric, such as denim, canvas, or felted wool.

EXTRA BOBBINS

I always keep extra empty bobbins on hand so that when I start a new project, I can wind several bobbins with thread right away. Then when I'm stitching my project, I don't have to interrupt my momentum to wind them.

Pressing Tools

IRON

A very hot iron is essential for pressing cotton fabrics, so they're crisp and wrinkle-free. Most new standard-sized irons will get hot enough for cotton, so your iron need not be expensive. After several years of use, though, irons tend not to get as hot as they did when new, so expect to buy a new iron every couple years. I have used irons by both Black and Decker and Rowenta and recommend both.

SPRAY BOTTLE

Instead of using the steam feature on my iron, I prefer to use a spray bottle to dampen my fabric before pressing. Sometimes the water build-up in an iron can stain fabric, especially if you leave the water in your iron indefinitely.

Quilting and Binding Tools

MASKING TAPE

I always keep plenty of 2-inch-wide masking tape around when I'm preparing a quilt's backing fabric for basting (see page 147). You can use a tape that's wider than 2 inches, but don't use a narrower one since it won't hold the fabric securely. And don't skimp on tape as you work: The back of your quilt needs to be taped down sufficiently to ensure that your basting is successful.

BENT-ARM SAFETY PINS

Bent-arm safety pins look like regular safety pins, but their bent arm makes them much easier to use for pin-basting (see page 147). This is because your quilt is usually taped or clamped down to a work surface as it's basted, and the bent arm of the pin allows it to be guided easily through the fabric layers and back to the quilt front. To close these pins, use a small, pointed tool like a knitting needle to lift the pin's arm into the catch. (You can't have too many of these safety pins. No matter how many I have, I always want a few more!)

QUILTING FRAMES

A quilting frame holds the three layers of your basted quilt together, freeing both your hands to hand-quilt. Quilting frames can be as small as 18 inches wide and as large as 120 inches wide, and they range in shape from circles and ovals to squares and rectangles. They're typically made of either wood or plastic, and can be free-standing or meant to sit in your lap. For the simple hand-quilting projects in this book, a lap-size frame is all you need. If you're new to hand-quilting, I recommend trying a 20-inch wooden, circular hoop and an 18-inch-square, plastic "snap-frame" to see which style and shape you prefer; both are relatively inexpensive.

When using a quilting frame, keep in mind that the fabric should be loose in the frame. The hoop is there merely to hold the fabric for you so that both your hands are free to work. If your fabric is stretched too tight, it will be very difficult to quilt.

TAPE MAKER

Tape makers quickly fold both raw edges of a fabric strip toward the center, so the resulting tape can be wrapped around and sewn over a quilt's raw edges to bind them. Tape makers are available in a variety of widths, from ¼ inch to 2 inches, and can be found at just about any fabric or quilt shop. It's very convenient to keep tape makers in a range of widths on hand.

To use a tape maker, cut your strip of fabric twice as wide as the tape maker's small end, and then feed the strip, wrong side up, through the large end of the tape maker. Pull about ½ inch of fabric through the tape maker's small end, making sure that the fabric isn't twisted, and pin the end of the newly folded tape to your ironing board with a safety pin. Pull the tape maker down the strip and away from the pin, ironing the strip immediately as it leaves the tape maker.

HEM CLIPS

Hem clips look like hair barrettes but are used to hold the binding in place while you sew it to the back of your quilt. Most quilt shops sell these clips in packets of ten, which is more than enough. To use hem clips, place two or three along the binding about 3 inches apart.

Miscellaneous Tools

SEAM RIPPER

Occasionally you'll make mistakes when piecing fabrics. Luckily, there are very few mistakes that can't be fixed if you have a good-quality seam ripper.

A seam ripper is essentially a handle with a blade that's tiny enough to fit underneath your stitches. This simple tool is an absolute necessity for quilting; and the sharper and finer its point, the more efficiently it works. I like the Clover seam ripper because of its extra-fine, sharp point.

To use a seam ripper, cut the thread of every third or fourth stitch on one side of your seam. Then pull out the thread on the opposite side of the seam, where it should remain in one piece. Finally, remove the remaining small bits of cut thread.

TWEEZERS

A sharp pair of tweezers is very useful for picking out threads from a ripped seam or stray threads on the front of your quilt. Tweezers are easily found in most drugstores and are also sold in some needlework stores.

LINT REMOVER

I use a lint remover to lift stray threads from fabric, especially any threads on the wrong side of a quilt top that I am about to baste (if they remain there, they'll show through the finished quilt). I like to use a masking tape-style lint roller, and I've found that the ones pet stores sell have the stickiest tape.

TECHNIQUES

There are hundreds of techniques for patchwork and quilting, each one meant to achieve a goal, such as refining your results, saving time, and creating greater efficiency as you sew. In this section, I've included the techniques that I rely on most often. Since I'm frequently in a hurry when it comes to making things, including last-minute gifts, I usually stick to the simplest and most direct techniques. If you want to learn more about quilting techniques, start by taking a look at the books listed on page 154.

Preparing Fabrics

When I come home with a new fabric, I immediately throw it in the laundry basket so that it gets washed before it sees the inside of my sewing room. Once it's washed and dried, I press it, even if I'm not going to use it right away. That way, if I want to make a last-minute gift with it, I just have to touch it up with an iron before diving in.

PREWASHING

Prewashing your fabrics shrinks them and dissolves any excess dye or chemicals leftover from the manufacturing process. Prewashing makes finished projects easier to care for and also softens fabrics, making them nicer to handle while you're sewing. I recommend machine-washing your fabrics with the same cycle and detergent that you would use for the finished project.

I hear over and over again how contemporary dyes and printing techniques create colorfast fabrics that do not bleed when you wash them, but I still don't find them to be 100-percent stable. I've seen brand new fabrics bleed time and time again, ruining a quilter's hard work; so, please, prewash your fabrics!

BLEED TEST

One way to ensure that your fabrics will not run or bleed once they become part of a project is to do a bleed test. This test is especially important if you're using vintage fabrics (those approximately 20 years old or older), which tend to bleed and run much more than contemporary fabrics. To do a bleed test, first wash and dry your fabric. Then dip a corner of the fabric in some water (the temperature doesn't matter). Squeeze the wet end of your fabric in a white paper towel; if the paper towel shows dye from your fabric, it will bleed when you wash it. You can try prewashing your fabric a few times, if necessary, to keep it from bleeding. But if, on repeated bleed tests, it continues to run, consider replacing the fabric with another option.

DRYING

After prewashing, machine-dry your fabrics on a normal setting. Keep in mind that you aren't trying to prevent the fabric from shrinking or bleeding when you prewash and dry. In fact, if the fabric is going to bleed or shrink, you want it to happen at this stage *before* you sew with it. A project made with prewashed and dried fabric is very easy to care for. Just pop it in the washer and dryer on a normal setting.

PRESSING

Pressing fabrics for patchwork and quilting is a little different from ironing clothing. When you press patchwork, you press your fabric flat. You don't pull or stretch it in any way. The goal is to keep the grain of the fabric's weave straight as you press, so the pieces cut from the fabric will retain their shape once you've sewn and washed your project.

Because I find that using a steam setting on the iron sometimes causes my fabric to swell and buckle, I usually dampen my fabric with mist from a spray bottle and then press it with a completely dry iron. The highest heat setting on an iron is usually appropriate for linens and cottons, a medium setting for wool or silk, and the lowest setting for synthetics.

Cutting Fabrics

Every project in this book is pieced by machine. When you cut fabrics for machine-piecing, the accuracy of the cut edge is important because that edge will become your guide when sewing. I recommend using a rotary cutter for making straight cuts and a very sharp pair of fabric scissors for curved cuts.

When I teach beginning quilting, I find that most students are intimidated by the rotary cutter (especially after I make clear how dangerous it can be — see safety tips at right). If you're new to rotary cutting, I highly recommend that you practice on some muslin before starting a project. Also, don't be shy about asking for a mini-lesson in rotary cutting at your local quilt shop.

STRUCTURED ROTARY CUTTING

Most of the projects in this book call for cutting the fabrics in a particular way to a given set of dimensions, which involves squaring up the fabric and cutting with rulers, as described in the steps that follow. By contrast, a few of the projects call for cutting freehand, that is, without rulers, which is explained on page 141. In both cases, make sure that you've pressed your fabric nice and flat before making any cuts.

ROTARY CUTTER SAFETY

Rotary cutters are excellent tools and make cutting fabric easy and neat, but they can be very dangerous if not handled properly. Below are some safety guidelines to follow:

* Choose a rotary cutter with a safety mechanism that draws the blade in when you're not squeezing the handle.

* Lock the blade in the safety position whenever you put the rotary cutter down.

* Use a sharp blade so that you don't need excessive pressure when cutting, which can be dangerous if your focus slips while you cut.

* Always cut away from your body.

* Keep your rotary cutter out of the reach of children at all times.

Step 1. Fold Fabric Selvage to Selvage

Fold your pressed fabric from selvage to selvage (the selvages are the tightly woven edges, about ¼ inch wide, that run along each side of the fabric), and carefully align the selvage edges. Don't be concerned if your selvages don't line up exactly; they often don't after washing and pressing. Do not press the fold because that can distort the fabric. Lay the fabric on your cutting mat with the fold nearest you and the selvages facing away from you.

To cut straight pieces, always measure from the folded edge, so the pieces won't end up crooked in the center when unfolded. I don't worry much about cutting exactly on the fabric's straight grain (which runs along the fabric's length). I think the slight puckering caused by a cut that's a tiny bit off-grain gives patchwork a handmade charm.

Step 2. Square Up With Two Rulers

(Note: The following is written for right-handed people; if you're left-handed, set your rotary cutter for left-handed cutting, and reverse these instructions.)

Once you wash and press your fabric and align the selvage edges, the fabric's cut edges will probably be slightly askew. The first cut you make to your fabric is called "squaring up," and its purpose is to make your cut edges parallel to one another and at a 90-degree angle to the fabric's fold so that the additional cuts you make will produce long, straight pieces.

To square up your fabric, you'll need a 6½-inch x 24½-inch ruler for cutting and another ruler for squaring up (I prefer a 12½-inch square ruler). Position your squaring-up ruler on the fabric about 1 inch from the left cut edge of the fabric (which is perpendicular to the fold) and 1 inch below the fold; then align the ruler's markings with the fabric's fold as precisely as possible. Hold the squaring-up ruler in place with your right hand. With your left hand, place your 6½-inch x 24½-inch ruler snug up against the left edge of the squaring-up ruler and over the 1 inch of fabric at the left edge of the squaring-up ruler (see the photo at right). Hold the ruler you just positioned firmly in place, and re-move the squaring-up ruler.

Cut across the fabric with your rotary cutter, using the ruler's long edge as a guide and beginning just below the fabric's fold. Walk your left hand up the ruler as you cut to keep it from slipping against the pressure of the rotary cutter. The fabric's left edge should now be perfectly square to the fold of your fabric.

Step 3. Make First Cuts, Selvage to Selvage

Once you've squared up your fabric, make your first cuts from left to right measuring with your 6½-inch x 24½-inch ruler from the fabric's left edge. Make subsequent cuts along the left edge from the fold toward the selvages.

A few of the patterns (such as Summer Breeze on page 95) require you to make first cuts that run parallel, rather than perpendicular, to the selvages. For these projects, follow the directions for folding the fabric as described in the pattern, and then proceed with your cuts from left to right, as explained above. The only difference will be that you'll be cutting your strips parallel to the selvages rather than perpendicular to them.

Squaring Up: Use two rulers to square up your fabric for cutting strips. The ruler on the right-hand side is to square up the bottom edge of the fabric. The ruler on the left will be the straight edge to guide the rotary cutter. In this photo, I am preparing to cut off the left edge of the fabric underneath the rulers.

Step 4. Trim Selvages

Once you've cut your strips, you'll trim the fabric's selvages. Gently turn your strips, so they run horizontally on your cutting mat, with the selvages to the left. (When you move your strips, the goal is to keep the piece as straight as possible, so handle the strips with care.) Place your squaring-up ruler on the strips, about 2 inches to the right of the selvages, and square up the left edge of your strip by aligning the ruler's markings with both cut edges of your strip. Hold the ruler in place with your right hand. With your left hand, place your 6½-inch x 24½-inch ruler snug up against the left edge of your squaring-up ruler and over the selvages. Hold the left ruler firmly in place, and remove your squaring-up ruler. Cut the fabric with your rotary cutter, beginning just below the fabric's horizontal edge and using the ruler's edge as a guide. If you're planning to make further cuts, don't move the strip.

Step 5. Make Second Cuts

If your project directions call for making second cuts to your strips, make these cuts the same way you made the first cuts, from left to right, measuring from the left-hand edge of your fabric with your ruler.

FREEHAND ROTARY CUTTING

There are a couple projects in this book (Stacked Coins on page 98 and (Sort of) Crazy Quilt on page 117) that recommend using your rotary cutter to cut "freehand." Cutting freehand simply means cutting fabric strips without using a straight-edge ruler to guide your cuts. Freehand rotary cutting is a great way to make irregularly shaped pieces, and it's also very efficient. When you cut freehand, be sure to follow the same safety guidelines given for rotary cutting. Always cut away from your body and always use a sharp blade.

CUTTING WITH SCISSORS

I like to cut curved shapes with scissors instead of a rotary cutter. If you keep your scissors sharp, you should be able to cut though several layers of fabric at a time without distorting the fabric's shape. To cut with scissors, first trace the shape on the fabric with a pencil, and then cut exactly on the drawn line.

Pinning

Some people think it's a waste of time to do a lot of pinning, but I find exactly the opposite to be true! The more carefully I pin, the more accurate my sewing, the less time I spend ripping out seams, and the better my cut pieces will fit together.

I usually place my pins about 1½ to 2 inches apart, or closer if I'm trying to fit together pieces that aren't precisely the same size or shape. Unless I'm working with especially heavy fabric, I prefer to use very fine pins with glass heads (see page 134).

I never sew over my pins, and I recommend that you don't either since it can be dangerous! If your needle hits a pin at high speed, the needle can snap and break, potentially flying into your eye. The few seconds you "save" by sewing over your pins just isn't worth it.

BASIC PINNING

Begin by carefully aligning the corners and edges of the cut pieces you're pinning together. Place a pin about ¼ inch in from each corner and another pin in the center. Then place a pin between each pin. Continue adding pins between pins until your pins are no more than 1½ to 2 inches apart. Extend the pins' heads beyond the fabric's edge by about ½ inch to make them easy to pull out when you sew.

LINING UP SEAMS

If you're pinning together pieces with intersecting seams, first carefully line up the seams, and place a pin on each side of the seam through the seam allowances, as shown in the photo below. Then line up the corners of your pieces and pin them. Continue adding pins between each pin, as explained above.

Lining Up Seams: Pin intersecting seams first through both sides of the seam allowance, and then pin corners. Place subsequent pins in between until pins are approximately 1½ - 2 inches apart.

Sometimes the pieces you've cut don't align perfectly, so that, after pinning the corners, you may find one edge a little longer than the other. Because woven fabric has a little stretch or "ease," you can usually solve the problem by adjusting the way you place your pins: Once you've pinned the corners, give them a slight tug in opposite directions to gently ease the fabrics together. Keep the fabrics gently stretched, and place a pin in the center. Continue adding pins between the center and corner pins, keeping the fabrics gently stretched to spread out the ease. When you sew a seam that involves a lot of stretching, go slowly, and sew just up to each pin before removing it; this helps prevent pleats and tucks in your seam.

Sewing

All the projects in this book are sewn primarily by machine, with several of them finished with hand-sewn stitches. Following are sewing techniques that will help you complete these projects efficiently.

MEASURING SEAM ALLOWANCES

A seam allowance is the width of the fabric from the stitched seam to the cut edge, and the width of a seam allowance can vary, depending on the project and the designer's wishes. If there's one thing to be really picky about when sewing, it's making sure your seam allowance measurements are accurate (that is, they match the measurement called for in the pattern).

Almost every pattern in this book is written for a ¼-inch-wide seam allowance. If your seam allowance is larger than ¼ inch, your sewn pieces will turn out smaller than required. If your seam allowance is smaller than ¼ inch, your joined pieces will turn out larger than they should be. In either case, the pieces won't fit together properly. You can save yourself a huge headache by taking time to get acquainted with your machine and find out exactly how wide a ¼-inch seam allowance is.

Many machines come with a ¼-inch foot, whose edge is precisely ¼-inch away from the needle so that you can easily align the fabric's cut edges with the edge of the

foot to sew ¼-inch-wide seams. As well, the needle plate (the flat metal plate that the needle moves down into) on many machines has ¼-inch, ½-inch, and ⅝-inch guide-marks to help you position the fabric for various seam widths. If your machine doesn't have a ¼-inch foot or needle plate guide-marks, and you're unsure of where to position the fabric's edges to make a ¼-inch seam, try sewing some seams and measure the allowances. If necessary, mark a ¼-inch guideline on the machine's needle plate with masking tape or a permanent marker.

BACKSTITCHING

If you've ever sewn a garment by machine, you're probably familiar with backstitching. It involves sewing a few stitches in reverse at the beginning and end of the seams in order to keep the ends of these seams from unraveling.

If you've never pieced a quilt on a machine, you may be surprised to learn that you almost never need to backstitch seams. This is because, in patchwork, you'll generally be sewing a seam that intersects another seam, even if you're joining a piece to an edge (you'll sew an intersecting seam on the edge when you attach the binding). Also, unlike on most garments, the seams on a quilt won't be subjected to a lot of stress and wear and tear, and therefore don't need the extra strength that backstitching provides for garment seams.

Nonetheless, there are a few projects in this book that do call for backstitching, for example, On Pins + Needles (page 19), Pieced Pillows (page 37), and Happy Birthday Pillow (page 58). Your machine should have a button or lever to press to make a few stitches in reverse. If it doesn't, you can hand-turn the machine's flywheel in reverse to backstitch.

To backstitch at the beginning of a seam, start a couple stitches in from the edge of your fabric, press the backstitch button (or start hand-turning the flywheel in reverse) to sew a few backstitches. At the edge of the fabric, release the backstitch button or flywheel, and sew forward as usual.

To backstitch at the end of a seam, sew to the seam's end, press the backstitch button or manually start turning the flywheel in reverse, and take from three to five backstitches. If you're sewing on a particularly loose woven fabric, you can also set the machine to a shorter stitch length (see your machine manual) before backstitching for extra security.

CHAIN-PIECING

Chain-piecing is a wonderful time-saving way to do the preliminary piecing of the cut fabrics for patchwork. It has the added benefit of keeping your pieced fabric organized while you're sewing. It involves sewing together pairs of cut pieces continuously without lifting the presser foot or cutting the threads.

The best way to start chain-piecing is to begin with what's called a "lead fabric." The lead fabric is just a scrap that you use to avoid having threads tangle or knots form on your actual pieces, which sometimes happens when you first start sewing on any fabric. Using a lead fabric also enables you to begin sewing exactly on the edge of your actual piece, so your seam will be perfectly finished on both ends.

Chain-piecing: To save time when sewing several patchwork pieces, just sew across the fabric pieces without lifting the presser

To chain-piece, first sew across your lead fabric, and, without lifting the presser foot or cutting the thread, place the first pair of cut pieces to be joined in front of the presser foot, and sew across their pinned edge. At the end of that seam, place the next pair of pieces in front of your presser foot, and repeat the process, continuing like this until you've joined all your cut pieces. Cut the threads between the sewn pairs, press the seams (see left), and set the lead fabric aside for future use.

STRIP-PIECING

Almost every quilt in this book is strip-pieced, that is, cut and sewn in strips. Strip-piecing, along with rotary cutting and chain-piecing, helps save time. When I buy fabrics for piecing, I almost always prefer to buy yardage rather than fat-quarters (see page 128). While fat quarters are a great resource, especially when you don't need a lot of fabric, I find that they often end up requiring more cutting and sewing of smaller pieces than yardage.

Most of the project instructions in this book tell you to cut the fabrics in strips, sew them together in a particular order, and then cut them again in specific ways to create smaller pieces. Of course, there are endless ways to construct almost any quilt, and certainly there are ways of cutting that enable you to get more square inches out of each piece of fabric. So if my way of cutting doesn't appeal to you, don't be afraid to experiment. Personally, I love to generate big, usable scraps, especially when there are two or more pieces already sewn together. These oversized scraps are among my best resources for smaller projects, exploring color relationships, and testing out other ideas.

PRESSING SEAMS

Quilters seem to be split into two groups on the subject of pressing seams: those who press their seams open and those who press their seams to one side. Most of the time I like pressing seams to one side because it's quick, eliminates show-through when the lighter-color fabric is pressed to the side of the darker fabric, and prevents the quilt batting from escaping between the stitches.

To press your seam to one side, place your pieced pair of fabrics on the ironing board with the darker of the two fabrics on top and the open edge facing you. Peel back the darker fabric as you press the lighter fabric underneath it. Then pull the darker fabric back taut, and move the edge of your iron that's still on the lighter fabric firmly against the seam. Finally, let go of the edge of the darker fabric, and press it flat, too. Your two seam allowances should now be neatly pressed to the side of the darker fabric.

If you're piecing a complex pattern with lots of intersecting seams and the pattern does not say which side to press the seams to, pressing your seams open is a good alternative, though it takes more time. To press seams open, work from the fabric's wrong side and open the seam with your fingers; then press the seam allowances flat with your iron. Then turn your piece right side up and press the seam again to finish.

FINGER-PRESSING

Occasionally when sewing, you'll need to make a quick crease in your fabric or fold a seam allowance to the opposite side to align the seams. The quickest and easiest way to do this is press a crease or seam with your fingers. To finger-press, simply fold the piece as required and run your finger over the crease or seam a few times.

TURNING A PROJECT RIGHT SIDE OUT

When you sew a project right sides together—that is, inside out—you'll need to turn it right side out to finish it. Although this is pretty straightforward—simply pull the project right side out through the remaining seam opening, as specified in the pattern—there are a few things to keep in mind: If your project has corners or a sharp point on it, before turning the project right side out, it's helpful to trim the seam allowances at the corners or point to about ⅛ inch to reduce bulk. If you trim these allowances any closer to the seam, you risk having the stitches pull apart once you turn the project.

To get crisp corners and points, it's also helpful to use a small blunt turning tool (I use the non-hook end of a small crochet hook) to gently poke the corners and points out from the inside. If you have trouble turning out your corners or points completely, use a straight pin on the right side to gently coax them outward; then, from the inside, poke the corner or point again with your turning tool.

Hand-Sewing

Even if you intend to sew everything by machine, there are occasional projects that call for sewing or finishing a few details by hand. Below are the hand stitches that you'll need. For all these stitches, unless otherwise noted, thread a hand-sewing needle with an 18-inch length of thread and tie a quilter's knot (see page 149) in one end. At the end of your stitching, tie a small knot in the thread, push the needle through the fabric near the last stitch, then back out about ½ inch away, pull the needle to pop the knot inside, and trim the thread tail.

BLINDSTITCH

Use a blindstitch to invisibly close a seam opening from the right side or to finish stitching a double-fold binding (see page 151) to the back of a quilt. To prepare to close a seam opening, press the opening's seam allowances to the wrong side, using the seam-allowance width given in the pattern. To prepare to finish a double-fold binding, fold the binding to the back of the quilt and blindstitch as follows:

1. Draw the needle up from the wrong side through the seam allowance, just short of the fold, and pull the thread taut.

2. Take a tiny (⅛ inch or less) horizontal stitch in the opposing seam allowance, again a hair's width below the fold, and pull the thread taut.

3. Take a small horizontal stitch just below the fold of the opposite seam allowance, about ⅛ inch from the previous stitch on that side. Repeat this step to close your seam fully.

OVERHAND STITCH

An overhand stitch is made with close, tiny stitches that pass over a seam or edge being closed or hemmed. This stitch is much quicker than a blindstitch for finishing a seam opening from the right side, but it's also much more visible. To prepare to close an opening with an overhand stitch, press the opening's seam allowances to the wrong side, using the seam-allowance width given in the pattern. Then sew as follows:

1. Draw the needle from the wrong side up through the fold of the seam allowance, and pull the thread taut.

2. Pass the needle over the seam, and draw it through the folds of both seam allowances.

3. Pass the needle over the seam again, draw it through the fold of both seam allowances about ⅛ inch from the previous stitch. Repeat this step until you've closed the seam.

BACKSTITCH FOR EMBROIDERY

This stitch, worked from right to left, is used to outline the letters on Happy Birthday Pillow (see page 58).

1. Bring the needle up from the back of the fabric where you want to begin (Point 1). Insert the needle ⅛ inch behind Point 1, bring the needle back out ⅛ inch in front of Point 1, and pull the thread taut to form the first stitch.

2. To make the second stitch, insert the needle just ahead of the first stitch, and bring it back out about ⅛ inch in front of where the thread exits the fabric, and pull the thread taut. Repeat as needed for your embroidery.

3. Tie off the thread on the back of the work by slipping the needle underneath the stitches. Trim the thread tail.

RUNNING AND GATHERING STITCHES

The running stitch is a simple, short, even stitch that can be used for quilting (as in the Washed Silk Quilt on page 110) and, when lengthened, can be used for gathering or closing a seam opening with gathers, as it does in Peanut, the Wee Elephant (see page 68). For both stitches, thread a needle with an 18-inch length of thread; and knot the thread with a quilter's knot (see page 149) for the running stitch, but do *not* knot it for the gathering stitch. Make these stitches as follows:

1. To make running stitches, run the needle in and out of the fabric to create small stitches that are the same length and evenly spaced. To make gathering stitches, lengthen the running stitches and the spaces between them to about ¼ inch.

2. For a gathering stitch, pull the thread from each end, so the fabric bunches up between the stitches.

3. End a line of running stitches by tying a small knot in the thread, pushing the needle through the fabric near the last stitch, then back out about ½ inch away, pull the needle to pop the knot inside, and trim the thread tail. End a line of gathering stitches by tying off each end of the thread with a square knot (pass the thread right-over-left and then left-over-right), and then trimming the thread tails.

Finishing Your Quilt

After you've completed your quilt top, there are a few steps involved to complete the project: making the quilt sandwich (that is, layering the quilt top, batting, and quilt back), basting the sandwich to stabilize it for quilting, quilting the layers, squaring up the quilt, and binding its edges.

MAKING A QUILT SANDWICH

Taking the time to make your quilt sandwich properly will make quilting your project much easier. Depending on the size of your workspace, you can make your quilt sandwich all at once or work on it one section at a time.

Working All at Once

I usually make my quilt sandwich on the floor, so I can do it all at once. And even though working on the floor is hard on the knees, I prefer this way because it's quicker than making a quilt sandwich in sections.

Step 1. Smooth Out Quilt Back

After making sure your work surface is clean, lay your quilt back right side down. Using 2-inch-wide masking tape, begin taping the center of each side to the work surface. Pull the fabric taut as you tape to smooth it completely, but don't pull it so tight that you actually stretch it. Once you've taped each side's center, start taping out toward each corner, alternating sides as you work to keep the fabric smooth but unstretched. Once taped down, the back should be completely smooth.

Step 2. Lay Down Batting

Take the batting out of its packaging, open it up, and fold it into fourths. Place the corner with two folds in the approximate center of your quilt back, unfold the batting into place, and gently smooth it out from the center. Handle the batting with care to prevent tearing or puncturing it. If your batting is larger than the quilt back, trim it down with scissors, so at least 1 inch of the quilt back shows on all sides.

Step 3. Lay Down Quilt Top

Fold your quilt top into fourths, with right sides together. Lay the corner with two folds in the center of the batting, and unfold the top into place, so it's right side up. Smooth it out gently from the center. Be sure your batting extends beyond the quilt top by about 4 inches on all sides to ensure that there will be batting behind the entire quilt top when you baste the quilt.

Working in Sections

If you don't want to make your quilt sandwich on the floor, you can work on a tabletop. The larger your table, the quicker this process will go. Before beginning, be sure that your batting is either the same size as your quilt back or only 1 inch smaller than the back on each side. This setup enables you to visually check to see that there's batting behind the entire quilt top before you begin basting the sandwich.

Step 1. Smooth Out Quilt Back

Lay your quilt back right side down on the center of your table, so the back's center is aligned with the table's center in both directions. Begin by securing the center of each side to the table's surface with office binder clips (or with masking tape if your quilt is narrower than the table in one or both directions), pulling the fabric taut enough to smooth it completely but not so taut that you're actually stretching it. Once you have the center of each side secured, work out toward the corners, binder-clipping or taping the sides and alternating opposite sides as you work.

Step 2. Lay Down Batting and Quilt Top

Fold the batting into fourths, place it on the center of your quilt back, and smooth it out as explained in Step 2 of directions for Working All at Once. Then unfold the quilt top into place, right side up, and gently smooth it out from the center, as explained in Step 3 of Working All at Once.

Step 3. Basting in Sections

Once the section of your quilt top covering the table is in position, follow the basting instructions below for either pin-basting or thread-basting. Then, after basting that section, remove the clamps and/or tape from all sides; and move the quilt, so the basted area hangs off the side of the table, leaving 1 or 2 inches of the basted area on the tabletop. Carefully roll up the batting and unbasted quilt top to expose the quilt back, and secure the exposed back to the table as before. Unroll the batting and top, and smooth them out. Baste this section as you did for the first one, and repeat these steps to finish basting the quilt sandwich.

BASTING THE QUILT SANDWICH

Basting is a way to temporarily secure the three layers of your quilt sandwich before quilting it. If done well, basting ensures that all the layers are stable, makes the quilting process easier, and improves results. There are two types of basting: pin-basting, the quickest method but not recommended for hand-quilting (since the pins get in the way of the quilting frame), and thread-basting, which takes longer but can be used with both hand- or machine-quilting.

Pin-Basting

The drawback of this very quick method of basting is that you have to stop and start a lot while quilting to take out the pins since you cannot sew over them. To prepare for pin-basting, gather and open your bent-arm safety pins (see page 136). Pin the three layers of your quilt sandwich together in the center. Then pin outward in concentric circles no further than 3 inches apart. (To save time, I usually insert as many pins as I can in the area I can reach, then close all the pins at once, using a knitting needle to lift the pin's arm into the catch.) Pin all the way to corners and edges of your quilt sandwich to ensure that your quilt back doesn't flip under on itself when you begin quilting. Once you've finished pin-basting, remove the tape or clamps securing your quilt sandwich to the work surface, and you're ready to start quilting.

Thread-Basting

As I mentioned above, you need to thread-baste your quilt sandwich if you're planning to hand-quilt it. But since thread-basting takes far longer than pin-basting, why on earth would you want to thread-baste if you're planning on machine-quilting? Here are a few reasons: The pins can make a pin-basted quilt quite heavy and a bit unwieldy for quilting, especially if the quilt is large.

Also, with pin-basting, you have to stop and start often while quilting to remove the pins, slowing down the quilting process considerably. By contrast, with a thread-basted quilt sandwich, you can sew right over the basting stitches, which saves a lot of time, especially if you're planning to do a lot of quilting.

There are a lot of different styles of thread-basting, but I get the most stable results by starting in the center of the sandwich and basting outward in a spiral, keeping the stitching lines no more than 3 inches apart. You can also baste in a grid, or baste out in lines from the center in the shape of an asterisk.

To prepare for basting, thread your curved needle (see page 135) with the longest length of regular cotton sewing thread that you can pull through the quilt without it tangling (about 36 inches long) in a color that contrasts with both your quilt and your intended quilting thread. Do not knot the end of your thread since you'll want to be able to pull out the basting stitches easily after quilting.

With your quilt sandwich face up, begin by inserting your needle through the center of the sandwich, and take a first basting stitch through all three layers, pulling the thread back up to the quilt front and leaving about a 5-inch thread tail hanging loose. Stitch out in a spiral from the center, making stitches about 1 inch long and 1 inch apart. Continue stitching in a spiral, and when you have only about 5 inches of thread left, pull the needle off the thread and leave the thread tail loose. Repeat these steps to thread-baste the entire quilt.

Be sure to baste all the way to the corners and edges of your quilt sandwich, so your quilt back does not flip under on itself when you begin quilting. Once you've finished basting, remove the tape or clamps securing your quilt sandwich to the work surface.

QUILTING

There are lots of stitching designs for quilting, some very simple and some incredibly complex (take a look at the books on page 154 to learn more about complex quilting styles). Since I'm often in a hurry, I usually stick to straight lines, the simplest quilting design possible.

Many quilting books encourage you, after deciding on a quilting design for your project, to work on half of the quilt in one direction and then turn the quilt around to complete quilting the other half. I use a different method, not because that one isn't right, but because I've learned that, if I get locked into a quilting design that's stitched too close together from the beginning, I may never get my quilt finished! This is especially true when I have a finite amount of time to complete a project.

My allover-quilting method involves, first, stitching the broadest quilting design possible, then filling in between the broad pattern by halves all over the quilt. This means I have to take time to roll and unroll the quilt for machine-quilting or to move the hoop around the fabric for hand-quilting, but it also means that, in the end, I can decide to do less quilting than originally planned (provided my quilting is worked to at least the minimum spacing required by the batting manufacturer and noted on the packaging). I recommend allover-quilting for all the quilts in this book.

Machine-Quilting

Another one of my favorite ways to quilt is called "stitching-in-the-ditch," or stitching along the lines of my piecing seams. I like to think of it as "stitching-next-to-the-ditch" because I stitch just next to the seamline, not literally on top of it. I get very clean results by stitching on the side of the seamline without the seam allowances pressed under it (which is slightly lower than the other side with the seam allowances underneath) and at a distance from the seam that's about equal to my needle's width ($\frac{1}{32}$ inch or so). Stitching-in-the-ditch both highlights the quilt top's design and saves time: There's no need to mark the quilt before quilting since I will follow the existing seamlines in the quilt top's design.

If you're using a quilting design other than stitching-in-the-ditch, it's helpful to mark your quilting lines ahead of time. I always mark mine using a *hera* marker (see page 132) on the quilt top's right side. A simple grid or parallel lines are pretty quick to mark and work well on most quilts. If you've pieced a top that's based on a rectilinear grid and somehow your grid has gotten off-square, I recommend that you consider quilting it with a diagonal grid, which gives a similar effect and also camouflages the fact that your grid is off.

Preparing Your Quilt

Prepare for machine-quilting by first replacing the regular presser foot on your machine with the walking foot (see page 136), and thread the machine with regular cotton sewing thread. Next think about how you're going to fit the bulk of a large quilt under the narrow arm of your machine. The secret to doing this is rolling up both sides of the quilt, leaving just the area you want to quilt exposed. Usually you'll work from the quilt's center to the right, so the rolled side that has to fit underneath the machine's arm is never thicker than half of your quilt.

When you quilt, support the weight of the quilt by throwing its length (with the sides rolled in towards the center) over your left shoulder and allowing it to move smoothly forward towards the machine as you sew. Also support the weight of the quilt on the machine bed by gently pushing the fabric toward the walking foot and needle as you sew so that it looks slightly buckled ahead of the walking foot. This tactic enables the walking foot to take in the fabric evenly; and although it may seem counter-intuitive, I assure you that it will give you the best results. Pulling on your quilt or trying to stretch it out will produce uneven stitches and strain your machine.

Also consider the starting point of your quilting: If you're quilting from one edge across the design, rather than starting in the middle of the quilt, begin sewing on the exposed batting, so you don't have to backstitch. And when you come to the end of your stitching line, sew off the top's edge and onto the batting again.

If your quilting starts in the center of the quilt top, begin by securing your stitches in one of two ways: If your machine can be set to a very tiny stitch length (about 50 stitches per inch), begin by taking a few stitches at this length, then switch back to a regular stitch length (from 8 to 12 stitches per inch) to sew the quilting line. When you get near the very end of the quilting line, set your stitch length again for a tiny stitch, and sew a few stitches to secure your thread. Alternatively, if your machine cannot be set to such a small stitch length, begin and end your quilting lines with a few backstitches, stitching the rest of the quilting line at a regular stitch length.

Hand-Quilting

When you first try hand-quilting, you're likely to worry that your stitches are too big, but don't! As you work, just focus on getting even stitches, and your stitches will naturally become smaller and smaller as you get the hang of it. A hand-quilting stitch is simply a small running stitch (see page 145). I recommend learning what's called the rocking method (see below) for hand-quilting. Although this method can feel a bit awkward at first, it becomes a natural, easy motion with practice.

Using hand-quilting thread (see page 129), thread a bunch of quilting needles (see page 135) onto your spool before you start working. That way, when you run out of the thread as you're sewing, you don't need to fiddle with threading a new needle. You've already got several threaded and waiting on the spool; just pull the thread off the spool through the last needle on the thread, cut it, and get back to quilting.

I like to use a length of thread that's just shorter than my arm (about 18 inches) so that the thread won't wear down as it's repeatedly pulled through the fabric (as it would with a much longer strand), and I'm able to pull the whole length of the thread through in one movement. I sew with a single strand of thread, securing the end of it with a quilter's knot, which I consider magical (see right).

QUILTER'S KNOT

To make a quilter's knot, first cut a length of thread, around 18 inches long (or just shorter than the length of your arm). Thread a hand-quilting needle, and pull about 5 or 6 inches of thread through the needle's eye. Then follow the directions below:

1. Grasp the needle between your index finger and thumb.

2. With your other hand, pick up the opposite end of the thread.

3. Point the needle and the end of thread towards one another, and grasp the end of thread between the same thumb and finger holding the needle.

4. Using your other hand, wrap the thread around the needle two times (or three if you're using a very loose-woven fabric).

5. Pinch the wrapped thread with the fingers holding the needle.

6. Pull the end of the needle with the opposite hand while continuing to pinch the wrapped thread until the entire length of thread has passed through your fingers.

7. You should have a small knot near the end of your thread. (If you don't, it means that you weren't holding the wraps tight enough or close enough together. Keep trying until you get it— it won't take long.)

Step 1. Place Quilt in Quilting Frame

Place the section of the quilt sandwich you plan to quilt first in the frame. The quilt layers should be held very loosely in the frame, which is only there to help you hold the quilt so your hands don't get overworked.

Step 2. Insert Needle and Thread

After threading your needle and tying a quilter's knot, begin by inserting the needle on the front of your quilt about ½ inch from where you want to begin quilting, but don't push the needle through the back of the quilt. Instead, pull the needle up through the spot where you want to begin quilting, pull the thread taut and, with a light, quick tug, "pop" the knot to the inside of the batting.

Step 3. Quilt Using the Rocking Method

This method of quilting is very simple but can feel awkward to learn. The main point to keep in mind is that you're not holding the needle between your thumb and forefinger as you do to sew. In fact, try to keep your thumb out of it altogether!

In this method, you're quilting towards yourself as you work. Put your left hand under the quilt where you're going to begin. With your right hand, insert the needle's point into the fabric, perpendicular to the quilt, that is, straight down, not angled. Push on the end of the needle with your middle or index finger of your right hand through the quilt until it just grazes your left-hand finger underneath. (Always use a thimble on the pushing finger to protect it, and also wear one on the other finger underneath if the repetitive grazing is painful.) With the same finger on top, rock the needle backwards while pushing up with your left-hand finger to create a little bump on the fabric. With your right-hand finger, push the needle through the bump, so it comes out back on the top. Then pull the needle and thread up through the fabric, so the stitch just barely puckers it. Once you get the hang of it, you can load your needle up with many stitches at a time, or you can continue to make one stitch at a time and pull it through.

If your needle flies up in the air or snaps when you rock it back, your quilt is pulled too tight in the frame. The quilt should be loose enough in the frame so that you can move your needle freely without straining it.

When you're left with a few inches of thread, tie a knot as close to the fabric as you can; then push the needle back into the quilt near the last stitch, but don't go through the back of the quilt. Bring the needle out through the top about ½ inch away from your last stitch, and pull the needle and thread taut to pop the knot to the inside. Trim the thread tails, thread and knot a new needle, and start quilting again.

Tied Quilts

Another way to secure the layers of a quilt sandwich is to tie the quilt rather than quilt it. You'll need a sharp yarn needle (the smallest your yarn will go through) and some wool yarn (I don't recommend cotton since the knots come out too easily).

Use a pencil to lightly mark the places on your quilt where you want the ties to be (I usually place my ties on a 4-inch grid). Thread your needle with the longest length of yarn that you can pull through the quilt without tangling it (about 36 inches). Insert the needle where marked, sewing through all three layers. Bring the needle's point back out to the quilt front about ¼ inch away from where it went in, pull yarn through, leaving a 6-inch length of yarn. Stitch into the next mark through all three layers, bringing the needle back out to the front about ¼ inch from where it entered, and pull the yarn through, leaving about 12 inches of length between the first mark and the second. Continue stitching through the marks, leaving about 12 inches between them, until you run out of yarn.

Snip the yarn between marks, and tie the lengths in a square knot (wrap the ends right over left, then left over right). Cut down the excess yarn to your liking, but no shorter than 1½ inches. Repeat at each remaining mark to tie all of them.

SQUARING UP AND BINDING YOUR QUILT

Quilting will change the shape of your quilt, but if you squared up your fabric at the outset, made accurate cuts when sewing the quilt top, and saw that it was pretty much square before quilting it, then there's no need to trim off the top of the quilt to make it square. So squaring up the quilt at this point is really a matter of trimming off the excess batting and quilt back to match the dimensions of the quilt top. To do this, use the edges of your quilt top as a guide, place your ruler over each edge in turn, and trim off the excess with your rotary cutter. I usually wait to do this trimming until I've pieced my binding strips and am ready to sew the binding on (see below).

BINDING

You have two choices for binding your quilt: a double-fold binding or a machine-attached binding. I prefer the look of a double-fold binding, but sometimes a machine-attached binding makes more sense—it's much quicker! You can apply either binding to any quilt, but note that the two bindings require binding strips of different widths: A double-fold binding strip is cut 2¼ inches wide, while the machine-attached binding strip I prefer is cut 1¾ inches wide. The directions for piecing binding strips are the same for both bindings.

Piecing Binding Strips

To piece binding strips together to make one long continuous strip, start by laying out one cut strip of binding fabric horizontally, right side up. Lay a second strip, perpendicular to the first strip and right side down, over the first strip's right-hand corner, so the second strip extends down from the first. Align the corners of the two strips.

On the aligned corner, draw a diagonal line on the upper strip from the top left corner to the lower right corner of the bottom strip. Sew the strips together along this drawn line. Trim the corner to the right of the seam, leaving a ¼-inch seam allowance and cutting through both layers of fabric. Repeat this step to join the remaining strips, and press the seam allowances to one side. Make sure that the pieced strips are at least 12 inches to 15 inches longer than the quilt's circumference.

Double-Fold Binding, Mitered Corners: Sew strip to within ¼ inch of the corner. Remove from machine. Fold strip straight up and then straight down. Pin into place.

Sewing a Double-Fold Binding

Step 1. Attach Binding

Fold the pieced binding strip in half lengthwise, wrong sides together, but do not press the strip. Beginning in the middle of one long side on the quilt front, align and pin together the binding's doubled raw edges and the quilt's raw edges to within ¼ inch of the corner (see the top part of the photo above).

Start sewing the binding to the quilt with a ¼-inch seam allowance, beginning 5 inches from the starting edge of the pinned binding (so when you return to your starting point, you'll have enough extra, unattached binding fabric to finish the binding nicely). Stop sewing the binding when you're ¼ inch from the corner. Take a couple of backstitches, and remove the quilt and binding from the machine. Trim the thread tails.

Step 2. Make Mitered Corners

Turn the quilt so the edge with the sewn binding runs horizontally across the top (see the bottom part of the photo on previous page). Fold the binding strip perpendicular to the sewn section and away from blanket (straight up); then fold the binding strip perpendicular again, this time towards the quilt (straight down). The second fold should be even with the upper edge of the quilt. Pin the corner in place; then align, pin, and sew the binding's raw edges along the quilt's second side, again stopping ¼ inch from next corner. Backstitch at the end of this seam, and remove the quilt from the machine. Trim the thread tails.

Repeat the process of mitering and pinning the binding at the corners and sewing it to the remaining sides, stopping when you get 10 inches from where you began attaching the binding on the first side.

Step 3. Finish Ends

Unfold the loose ends of the binding strips. Fold under the end of the first strip ½ inch to the wrong side, and finger-press (see page 144) the fold in place. Lay the second strip on top of the first, and trim the second strip about 1½ inches longer than the first strip (trim the second strip's end diagonally to reduce bulk inside the seam).

Fold the second strip back in half lengthwise, and fold the first strip around the second strip, so it covers the second strip's raw end. Align, pin, and sew the four edges of the two strips folded together with the edge of the blanket. Backstitch at the end of the seam, and remove the quilt from the machine. Trim the thread tails.

Step 4. Hand-Stitch Back of Binding

You'll finish the binding by folding it to the other side of the quilt and hand-stitching it in place. The mitered corners should automatically fold into place nicely.

Thread a hand-sewing needle with a length of thread about 18 inches (or no longer than your arm). Make a quilter's knot (see page 149) at the thread's end.

Draw the needle down through the seam allowance on the back of the quilt, and then back up just a few threads outside of this seam allowance. Fold the binding to the back of the quilt, and secure it by blindstitching (see page 144) its folded edge every ⅛ inch around the quilt and picking up no more than two threads of the quilt back beyond the seam allowance with each stitch. Use an extra stitch at the mitered corners to anchor them securely. While sewing around the quilt, as you come to the end of your thread, knot and tie off the thread ends inside the seam allowance. Then anchor the knot of your new thread length in the seam allowance as well.

Machine-Attached Binding

For a machine-attached binding, you'll fold the binding strips with a tape maker (see page 137) to produce a perfectly folded strip, which you'll then fold around the raw edges of the quilt and machine-stitch in place (see the photo on next page). The trick for attaching this binding is being sure to sew through all folded-binding layers in one go. This can be challenging at first, so if you miss a few spots on the quilt back on your first attempt, just pull out the problematic part of the seam and do it again. The more you sew this kind of binding, the easier it will become.

Step 1. Press Binding

After piecing your 1¾-inch binding strips into one long strip at least 12 inches to 15 inches longer than your quilt's circumference, use a 1-inch bias tape maker to create a perfectly folded strip that you'll press immediately with your iron as you pull the fabric through the tape maker. Fold the strip one more time along its length to encase the cut edges, then press the crease into place.

Step 2. Attach Binding

Beginning in the middle of one long side of the quilt, pin the folded tape around the quilt's raw edges all the way to the corner. Then, working from the front of the quilt and beginning 5 inches in from the starting edge of the pinned binding (so when you return to your starting point, you'll have enough extra, unattached binding fabric to finish the binding nicely), sew the binding to

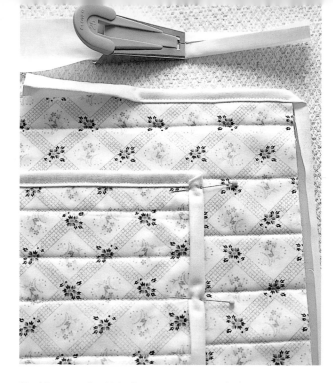

the quilt ⅛ inch from the tape's left edge. Be sure as you sew that you're simultaneously attaching both the folded front and back of the binding tape to the quilt. Sew the binding all the way to the corner, take a couple of backstitches, remove the quilt and binding from the machine, and trim the thread tails.

Step 3. Make Corner

Turn the quilt so that the edge with the sewn binding runs horizontally across the top and the loose end of the binding strip is at the right. Fold the binding strip straight down, with the two halves of the tape encasing the quilt edge. Pin the binding into place all the way to the corner (the binding will make a corner at the top that looks mitered). Sew as above, then backstitch, remove the quilt from the machine, and trim the threads. Repeat these steps to sew the binding to the remaining sides and corners. On the last side, sew to within 10 inches of where you began to attach binding and stop.

Step 4. Finish Ends

Unfold the loose ends of each binding strip. Then fold ½ inch of the first strip's end to the wrong side, and finger-press the fold in place. Lay the end of the second strip over the first strip, and trim the second strip to overlap the end of the first strip by about 1½ inches (trim the second strip diagonally to reduce bulk inside the seam). Fold the first strip around the second strip lengthwise, so its folded end covers the second strip's raw end. Pin the ends of the binding in place, and sew them to your quilt. Backstitch, remove the bound quilt from the machine, and trim the thread tails.

Machine-attached binding: Use a tape maker to make perfectly folded strips. For tidy corners, sew binding all the way to the corner, remove from machine, fold binding straight down and then fold it around the edge of the quilt.

RECOMMENDED READING
Patchwork and Quilting — Techniques + Patterns

Amy Butler's In Stitches
(Chronicle Books)
Amy Butler

Amy Butler has been on the scene for several years with her fabric and bag patterns. Her first book is an impressive resource of beautiful, practical patterns for sewing, patchwork, and quilt projects, each accompanied by easy-to-understand instructions. Find out more about Amy on her website www.amybutlerdesign.com.

Color Harmony for Quilts
(Rockport)
Weeks Ringle and Bill Kerr

This book includes excellent techniques and exercises that teach you to explore and enjoy color relationships in your quilts. You can learn more about the authors, two inspiring quiltmakers, at their website www.funquilts.com.

Denyse Schmidt Quilts
(Chronicle Books)
Denyse Schmidt

Denyse Schmidt is an innovative, modern quiltmaker who has been honing her unique style for years. In Denyse's first book, she shares her fresh and inspiring patterns. Learn more about Denyse at her website www.dsquilts.com.

Heirloom Machine Quilting
(C&T Publishing)
Harriet Hargrave

This is the most comprehensive and detailed book about machine-quilting I've ever read. In fact, Hargrave is one of the founding voices in the "machine-quilting revolution"; before she came along, the idea of quilting a quilt on a machine was almost unheard of. Hargrave includes everything from information on maintaining your sewing machine to masterful lessons on free-motion quilting.

The Modern Quilt Workshop
(Quarry Books)
Weeks Ringle and Bill Kerr

This is another invaluable resource from Ringle and Kerr for both designing and creating quilts with a contemporary flair. This book is a great technical guide for beginners and also offers clear direction for quilters of all levels who want to hone their design decisions and color choices and learn some innovative techniques.

Quilt Artistry: Inspired Designs from the East
(Kodansha International)
Yoshiko Jinzenji

Jinzenji is a fine artist who happens to be working in the medium of fabric. This book isn't just pretty pictures; it also includes patterns and how-tos for the inventive and unique techniques she has innovated while making her gorgeous quilts.

Quiltmaking by Hand
(Breckling Press)
Jinny Beyer

If you'd like to learn the authentic skills of quiltmaking by hand, Beyer's book is the best and most thorough resource I've ever encountered on the subject. This book covers everything from fabric to tools to hand-sewing to finishing. The last chapter includes complete patterns and directions for 10 of her original, lovely, hand-pieced projects.

Quilt Monographs — Inspiration

Amish: The Art of the Quilt
(Alfred A. Knopf)
Robert Hughes and Julie Silber

This is an incredible record of a collection of 82 quilts from Amish communities in Pennsylvania made between 1870 and 1950, curated by Julie Silber. Distinguished art critic Robert Hughes introduces the monograph with an elegant essay about looking at these quilts as a major American art form. The striking color photographs (one quilt per page) superbly capture the artistry of these quilts.

Amish Crib Quilts from the Midwest: The Sara Miller Collection
(Good Books)
Janneken Smucher, Patricia Cox Crews, and Linda Welters

The wonderful qualities of Amish quilts, plus a bit of whimsy, can be found in this tiny but excellent book. The small scale of these quilts seems to inspire their makers to be a little less formal in their designs, and yet the quilts retain the bold presence of their full-size counterparts.

Hawaiian Quilt Masterpieces
(Hugh Lauter Levin Associates, Inc.)
Robert Shaw

This book is a beautiful historical record of Hawaiian quilts made from 1874 to 1994, from amazing, giant appliqué patterns cut like paper snowflakes to the traditional flag quilts. Hawaiian quilts are a world unto themselves.

Nancy Crow
(Breckling Press)
Nancy Crow

This is a survey of Nancy Crow's ground-breaking work as an artist. Nancy is the founder of the "art quilt" movement in the United States. You can learn more about Nancy Crow's creative techniques and powerful style (and even sign up to take classes with her) at her website www.nancycrow.com.

The Quilts of Gee's Bend
(Tinwood Books)
Edited by William Arnett
& Paul Arnett

This is a poignant homage to the spirit of the Gee's Bend quilters. It includes hundreds of quilts from more than 100 quiltmakers working from the 1930s to the present. Gee's Bend is a small Alabama community geographically isolated by a winding river. Their strength, creativity, and ingenuity in the face of hardship make these inspired quilts even more remarkable. You can learn more about the quilts of Gee's Bend at their website www.quiltsofgeesbend.com.

SOURCES FOR SUPPLIES

Most of the fabric, batting, and tools featured in this book can be found at fabric stores and quilt shops nationwide and at:

Purl Patchwork
147 Sullivan Street
New York, NY 10012
(212) 420-8798
www.purlsoho.com

The batting for all of the projects in this book was provided by:

Quilter's Dream Batting
589 Central Drive
Virginia Beach, VA 23454
(888) 268-8664
www.quiltersdream batting.com

The printable cotton for all of the projects in this book was provided by:

The Electric Quilt Company
419 Gould Street, Suite 2
Bowling Green, OH 43402-3047
(800) 356-4219
www.electricquilt.com

Specialty Sewing and Craft Items

Most of the materials used in this book are available in stores that sell quilting supplies nationwide. Following are sources for the few items that might be harder to find.

PLANT-DYED WOOL FELT
(On Pins + Needles, page 19)
A Child's Dream Come True
1223-D Michigan Street
Sandpoint, ID 83864
(800) 359-2906
www.achildsdream.com

MOLESKINE CAHIERS JOURNALS
(Scrapbooks, page 30)
www.moleskineus.com
Also available at many large bookstores throughout the U.S.

PILLOW INSERTS
(Pieced Pillows, page 37, and Happy Birthday Pillow, page 58)
Artisana Works
P.O. Box 957
Bandera, TX 78003
(877) 441-550
www.Down-and-Feather.com

IRIDESCENT SILK TAFFETA
(Washed Silk Quilt, page 110)
B & J Fabrics
525 7th Avenue, 2nd floor
New York, NY 10018
(212) 354-8150
www.bandjfabrics.com

RED PEONY FABRIC
(Six of One, A Half-Dozen of the Other, page 80)
Pearl River Mart
477 Broadway
New York, NY 10012
(800) 878-2446
www.pearlriver.com

SNAP TAPE
(Pinwheel Duvet Cover, page 64)
Distributed by Blue Sky Alpacas
Blue Sky Alpacas
P.O. Box 88
Cedar, MN 55011
(888) 460-8862
www.blueskyalpacas.com

LINEN TWILL TAPE
(Colored Pencil Roll, page 48)
Bell'occhio
8 Brady Street
San Francisco, CA 94103
(415) 864-4048
www.bellocchio.com

Fabrics Used for Projects in This Book

Following is a list of the fabrics used for many of the projects in this book. Though we have tried to include as much information as possible, some projects simply use too many fabrics to list. It is also important to note that fabric manufacturers tend to introduce new fabrics and discontinue old ones quickly, so not all of these fabrics will necessarily be available. However, if you are looking for a particular fabric you see in this book, this list will help you to identify it and perhaps find it or at least one like it.

Less-Than-2-Hours

SIMPLE PILLOWCASES (page 23)
Printed floral fabric: Freespirit Fabrics, Amy Butler "Charm"

MADE-BY PATCH (page 29)
Quilt back fabric: Freespirit Fabrics, "Bohemian," Yellow Filigree Floral, #1463-505

2- to 4-Hours

FLANNEL BABY BLANKET (page 34)
Polka-dot binding fabrics: Michael Miller Fabrics, "Dumb Dot" in Candy, Coral, Kiwi, and Aqua

PIECED PILLOWS (page 37)
Dark brown fabric: Yuwa Fabrics, "Diamonds";
Red and pink solids: Robert Kaufman Fabrics, "Kona Cotton" in Bright Pink, Tangerine, Tomato, and Pomegranate

SIMPLE BAG (page 40)
Fabrics: Kokka Fabrics, Amy Butler's Forest Collection, "Grand Tapestry" and "Pods"

SUPER QUICK + EASY BABY QUILT (page 42)
White fabric with red stripe: Marcus Brothers Textiles, 19th-Century Backgrounds, "Crooked Stripes," #831-311T
Alphabet fabric: Lecien, Red and Blue Work Collection, #3576 WR

COLORED PENCIL ROLL (page 48)
Quilter's muslin: Moda Fabrics, Muslins;
Yarn-dyed cotton: Pinwheels Trading Company

4- to 8-Hours

PUZZLE BALL (page 54)
Dark fabric: Windham Fabrics, Fall River Collection, "Pin Stripe Dot," #24322-1; Light fabrics: Windham Fabrics, Fall River Collection, "Pin Stripe Dot," #24322-2, and Farmhouse Blues

Collection, "Black Diamonds," #24259-4 and "Black Ticking," #24263-4

PATCHWORK TABLECLOTH + NAPKINS (page 61)
Printed fabrics: Windham Fabrics, "China Blue," #24268-1 and "Dargate Prussian Blue," #24407-2 and #24414-2; Marcus Brothers Fabrics, "Old Sturbridge Village Blues," #698-121T and #695-121T

PINWHEEL DUVET COVER (page 64)
Floral print: Alexander Henry Fabrics, "Devora," #6550C; Off-white solid fabric: Moda Fabrics, Muslins, 108-inch muslin, natural

8- to 12-Hours

SIX OF ONE, A HALF-DOZEN OF THE OTHER (page 80)
Red peony fabric: See Specialty Sewing and Craft Items, opposite page

CUTTING CORNERS (page 86)
Center panel and outer border: Liberty of London, Tana Lawn, "Mirabelle," #6011d; Inner border: Windham Fabrics, Farmhouse Blues Collection, "Blue Dots," #24260-1; Second inner border: Robert Kaufman Fabrics, "Kona Cotton," sand; Binding fabric: P&B Textiles, "Color Spectrum," #CSPE 13 RO; Backing fabric: Robert Kaufman Fabrics, "Kona Cotton," lagoon

LITTLE BITS (page 90)
Dark brown background fabric: Quilt Gate "Silent Night," #SB71112R-20D
Various blue fabrics: Windham Fabrics, "China Blue," #24268-1 and "Dargate Prussian Blue," #24407-2 and #24414-2; Marcus Brothers Fabrics, "Old Sturbridge Village Blues," #698-121T and #695-121T; Back: Kokka Fabrics, "El Anche Antique Collection," #JA19000

SUMMER BREEZE
(page 95)
Green background fabric: Rowan Fabrics, Carla Miller Collection, "Geographea Dot Cube," #CM04, mint

STACKED COINS
(page 98)
Background fabric: P & B Textiles "Color Spectrum," #CSPE 12 YO

More-Than-12-Hours

FOLLOW-THE-LINES BABY QUILT (page 104)
Front: Alexander Henry Fabrics, "Ava," #6391C, pink; **Back:** Alexander Henry Fabrics, "Arvika," #6604B, pink; **Binding:** Robert Kaufman Fabrics, "Kona Cotton," tangerine

WASHED SILK QUILT
(page 110)
Backing and binding fabric: P&B Textiles, "Color Spectrum," #CSPE 33 Y; **Silk taffeta:** See B & J Fabrics, Specialty Sewing and Craft Items, page 156

LOG CABIN QUILT
(page 120)
Floral print: Freespirit Fabrics, Amy Butler "Charm"; **Off-white fabric:** Robert Kaufman Fabrics, "Kona Cotton," meringue

Fabric Distributors

To find a local source for the fabrics used in this book, contact the distributors below:

Alexander Henry Fabrics
1120 Scott Road
Burbank, CA 91504
www.ahfabrics.com

Freespirit Fabrics
1350 Broadway
21st Floor
New York, NY 10018
www.freespiritfabric.com

Kokka Fabrics
Seven Islands, Inc.
16921 South Western Avenue, #107
Gardena, CA 90247
www.kokka-usa.com

Lecien
(available through Kokka Fabrics)

Marcus Brothers Textiles, Inc.
980 Avenue of the Americas
New York, NY 10018
www.marcusbrothers.com

Michael Miller Fabrics
118 West 22nd Street
5th Floor
New York, NY 10011
www.michaelmiller fabrics.com

Moda Fabrics
13800 Hutton Drive
Dallas, TX 75234
www.unitednotions.com

P&B Textiles
1580 Gilbreth Road
Burlingame, CA 94010
www.pbtex.com

Pinwheels Trading Company
2006 Albany Post Road
Croton-on-Hudson, NY 10520
www.pinwheels.com

Quilt Gate
Available through Robert Kaufman Fabrics

Robert Kaufman Fabrics
129 West 132nd Street
Los Angeles, CA 90061
www.robertkaufman.com

Rowan Fabrics
Westminster Fibers
4 Townsend Avenue, Unit 8
Nashua, NH 03063
www.westminsterfibers.com

Windham Fabrics
812 Jersey Avenue
Jersey City, NJ 07310
www.baumtextile.com

Yuwa Fabrics
Kowa America
20001 South Vermont Avenue
Torrance, CA 90502

Machine-Quilting Services

When you just want someone else to finish your quilt, consider these services. They offer a number of different styles and patterns for quilting so you can customize your project. When planning your project, however, keep in mind that quilting services generally require four to six weeks' turnaround time.

The Little Red Quilt House
20 Wilson Street
Fairfield, CT 06825
(203) 258-9464
www.lrqh.com

The Threaded Pear
460 West Lambert Road
Suite A3
Brea, CA 92821
(714) 553-7389
www.threadedpear.com

ACKNOWLEDGMENTS

Writing has never come easily to me. I would like to thank my editor, Melanie Falick, for believing in my ability to create this book. Just as Melanie guided me through the writing of *Last-Minute Knitted Gifts*, she has helped me to bring this book to fruition. Without her to reassure me, look over my shoulder, and make sure I am actually expressing what I mean, *Last-Minute Patchwork + Quilted Gifts* would be nothing more than a dream. In addition to Melanie, I would like to thank editors Betty Christiansen, Cindy Young Forrest, Christine Timmons, and Liana Allday, who carefully read and gently edited my words as well.

I made the projects in this book with the calm assurance that they would be lovingly represented in beautiful photographs by my dear friend Anna Williams. Anna's work and friendship have inspired and influenced me for many years, and I feel incredibly blessed that she shares her vision with me. Throughout the creation of this book, Brooke Hellewell Reynolds generously contributed her time and outstanding imagination to almost every aspect of its development—from checking in on my project ideas and organizing my often chaotic process to participating in the photography to creating the lovely graphic design. She has become a good friend and trusted confidante. Kelly McKaig, another dear friend, not only created the wonderful pincushion pattern on page 45, but also stitched with me into the wee hours of the morning on more than one occasion to finish the projects in time for our photo shoots. I must also thank Kelly for rescuing the Washed Silk Quilt on page 110 from the scrap heap, where I put it after becoming convinced I couldn't finish it in time for photography. This book belongs to Anna, Brooke, and Kelly as much as it does to me.

I had been admiring the charming and unique work of Hillary Lang of www.weewonderfuls.com for some time before I thought to contact her about making a toy elephant for the book. I am sincerely grateful she agreed to contribute, even though she was in the throes of creating pattern books of her own. Her creation, Peanut, the Wee Elephant on page 68, is sure to become a cherished friend to many children. Similarly, I had been admiring Kathy Mack's Colored Pencil Roll on her website www.pinkchalkstudio.com for a long time from before I contacted her and I am very happy that she made time to write down her pattern so it could be reproduced here (see page 48).

Cassandra Thoreson, a long-time knitting customer at Purl and also an accomplished quilter who, in part, inspired my interest in patchwork and quilting, lovingly hand-quilted two projects: the (Sort of) Crazy Quilt on page 117 and Follow-The-Lines Baby Quilt on page 104. She literally gave life to these projects with her beautiful stitches, and I can't thank her enough—I will always treasure both. Cassandra also helped to finish several other quilts on these pages, while simultaneously teaching classes at Purl Patchwork.

During the creation of this book, my best friend, business partner, and sister Jennifer Hoverson and I opened Purl Patchwork (the sister store to our yarn store, Purl) and expanded our website (www.purlsoho.com) to include fabric and other patchwork and quilting supplies. Jennifer agreed to take the leap with me, knowing full well that I would be completely mired in the creation of this book while we worked to get our expanded business off the ground. Jen has toiled hard to get our shop inventories onto our website and, in the meantime, has developed a passion for quilting of her own. I'm thrilled that we share a love of making things. We couldn't have done any of it without the enormous contributions of our employees, George Czech, Nicole Egana, Phyllis Forbes, Isabelle Grizzard-Robertson, Jill Holthus-Servis, Leah Mitchell, Sasha Rockwell, Faye Rubenstein, Molly Montana Schnick, Whitney Van Ness, and Tracey Wallis, who ran the shops in my absence with tender love and care.

INDEX